†CROSSWALK

Robert Mackey

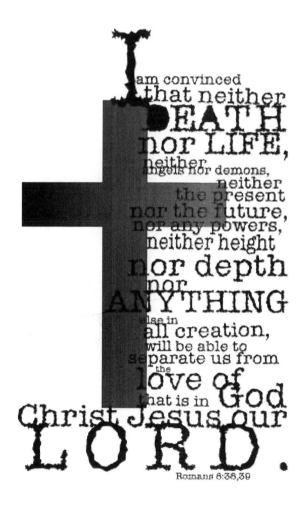

I am convinced that neither DEATH nor LIFE, neither angels nor demons, neither the present nor the future, nor any powers, neither height nor depth nor ANYTHING else in all creation, will be able to separate us from the love of God that is in Christ Jesus our LORD.

Romans 8:38,39

Published by Pathway Publications®, a unit of †Crosswalk
Ministry, P.O. Box 234, Broken Bow, OK 74728.

Printed in the United States of America.

ISBN-13: 978-1468129267

For all those brave enough to *follow* Jesus.

CONTENTS

PRAYER

Heavenly Father, I thank you for the unspeakable gift of your Son on the cross. I thank you for our eternal salvation, brought out by that death on the cross. He died for me that I might live eternally. Through His death on the cross I am dead to sin, and *live* in the power of His life.

Father please pour out the unending waters to teach me what it means that I am dead with *Christ* and can live my life in Him. Teach me to realize that my sinful flesh is corrupt and nailed to the cross to be destroyed, that the life of *Christ* may manifest in me as I *seek* to be one with Him.

INTRODUCTION

The question often arises how is it, with so much church-going, Bible-reading, and prayer, that the Christian fails to live the life of complete victory over sin and lacks the love and joy of the Lord. Has he forgotten about the cross of *Christ*? Does he not know what it is to *die* to himself and to the world? Yet, 'without this', God's love and holiness *cannot* have their dwelling place in his heart. He has repented of some sins, but doesn't know what it is to turn, not only from sin, but from his old nature and self-will.

This is what our Lord Jesus taught. He said to the disciples that if any man would come after Him, he must hate and lose his own life. He taught them to take up the cross. That meant they were to consider their life as sinful and under the sentence of death. They must give up themselves, their own will and power, and any goodness of their own. When their Lord had died on the cross, they would learn what it was to die to themselves and the world, and to live their life in the fullness of God.

Apostle Paul did not know *Christ* after the flesh, but through the Holy Spirit - *Christ* was revealed in his heart, and he could testify: "I am crucified with *Christ*; I live no longer; *Christ* lives [dwells] in me." In more than one of his epistles [letters] the truth is made clear that we are dead to sin, with *Christ*, and receive and experience the power of the new life through the continual working of God's Spirit in us each day.

As the seasons draw near each year, our thoughts will be occupied with the sufferings and death of our Lord Jesus *Christ*. Emphasis will be laid, in the preaching, on *Christ* for us on the cross as the foundation of our salvation. But, less is said about our death with *Christ*. It is a desire to help those who are considering this truth, that death to self and to the world is necessary for a life in the love and joy of *Christ*.

The great work of the Holy Spirit is to reveal *Christ* in our hearts and lives as the Crucified One who dwells within us. With complete dependence on God, and an expectation of continually receiving all goodness and salvation from Him alone. You will then learn to die to yourself and to the world, and will receive *Christ*, the Crucified and Glorified One, into your heart, and be kept through the continual working of the Holy Spirit.

You can read the Bible, go to church, and pray, but until you find your place at the foot of the *blood*stain cross, you will not know redemption and forgiveness for your sins.

All around us we see the compelling manifestations of man's degraded state. If we turn our eyes inward, we see our own personal corruption and degradation. Our exterior may be polished and pleasant, but inwardly our hearts are impure and unrighteous.

The apostle Paul quotes concerning man's inward state: "'There is none righteous, not even one; there is none who understands, there is none who seeks out God. All have turned aside; together they have become useless; there is none who does good; there is not so much as one.'" (Rom. 3:10-12, quoting Psa. 14:1-3)

Regardless of the seriousness of our offenses, *all* of them are our sins. These sins deserve and require punishment, especially in the eyes of God, who alone is righteous in this universe. Yet God's great love for man compelled Him to save man from punishment.

The requirements of His righteousness and the constraints of His love motivated God to save man in a way that only He could. This aspect of His salvation is accomplished by *Christ* as the Lamb of God. The Lamb of God is a symbol of Christ as the perfect offering for the sins of mankind. According to Isaiah, when *Christ* was dying on the cross,

God took *all* our sins and laid them upon this Lamb of God. In taking away our sin, the Lord did not simply *command* the sin to go away; on the contrary, on the cross He worked to pay our debt, to appease God, and to remove sin.

It is clear that we can *not* preach *Christ* without the cross.

THE CROSS

REDEMPTION BY CHRIST

"*Christ* redeemed us from the curse of the law, having become a curse for us." (Galatians 3:13)

Scripture teaches us that there are two points of view from which we may regard *Christ's* death upon the cross. One is the redemption of the cross: *Christ* dying for us as our complete deliverance from the curse of sin. The other, the fellowship of the cross: *Christ* taking us up to die with Him, and making us partakers of the fellowship of His death in our own experience.

The law of God has pronounced a curse on all sin and on all that is sinful. *Christ* took our curse upon Him - yes, became a curse - and so destroyed its power, and in that cross we now have the everlasting redemption from sin and all its power. The cross reveals to us man's sin as under the curse, *Christ* becoming a curse and so overcoming it, and our full and everlasting deliverance from the curse.

The lost and most hopeless sinner finds a sure ground of confidence and hope. God had indeed pronounced a curse upon this earth and all that belongs to it. On Mount Ebal, in connection with giving the law, most of the people of Israel had twelve reasons to pronounce a curse on all sin.

Twelve total curses were spoken from Mt. Ebal to correspond to the twelve tribes. And there was to be in their midst a continual reminder of it: "Cursed is every one who hangs on a tree."

The curse is an instrument of God's justice against the sin of His creatures. (Deuteronomy 21:23, 27:15-20) And yet who could ever have thought that the Son of God Himself would die upon the accursed tree, and become a curse for us? The very deed is the gospel of God's love, and the regretful sinner can now rejoice in the confident assurance that the curse is forever put away from all who believe in *Christ* Jesus.

The preaching of the redemption of the cross is the foundation and center of the salvation the gospel brings us. To those who believe its full truth it is the cause of continual thanksgiving. It gives us boldness to rejoice in God. There is nothing which will keep the heart more tender towards God, enabling us to live in His love and to make Him known to those who have never yet found Him. God be praised for the redemption of the cross!

God poured down from Heaven the judgment that should have fallen on us. Jesus bore our sins and suffered the penalty for them while He hung on that Cross.

The blood of *Christ* was shed for the forgiveness of sins, and the new covenant was accomplished with it. It guaranteed an eternal redemption for us and purchased the church for God. It cleans, sanctifies, purifies, and speaks something better for us. By the blood we overcome Satan!

We can never forget that the only reason we can receive anything from God and declare in faith "Amen" after a prayer is because Jesus said "Amen" to the curse and took our punishment upon Himself.

FELLOWSHIP BY SPIRIT

"Let this mind be in you which was also in *Christ Jesus.*" (Philippians 2:5)

Paul tells us what that mind was in *Christ*: He emptied Himself; He took the form of a servant; He humbled Himself, even to the death of the cross. It is this mind that was in *Christ*, the deep humility that gave up His life to the very death, that is to be the spirit that animates us. It is this that we shall prove and enjoy the fellowship of His cross.

Paul had said: "If there is any comfort in *Christ*," - the Comforter was to reveal His real presence in them - "if any fellowship of the Spirit," it was in this power of the Spirit that they were to breathe the Spirit of the crucified *Christ* and manifest His disposition in the fellowship of the cross in their lives.

As they strive to do this, they would feel the need of a deeper insight into their real oneness with *Christ*. They would learn to appreciate the truth that they had been crucified with *Christ*, that their "old man" had been crucified, and that they had died to sin in *Christ*'s death and were living to God in His life. They would learn that the crucified *Christ* lived in them, and that they had crucified the flesh. It was because the crucified Jesus lived in them that they could live crucified to the world.

And so they would gradually enter more deeply into the meaning and the power of their high calling to live as those who were dead to sin and the world and self. Each in his own measure would bear in his life the *marks* of the cross, with its sentence of death on the flesh, with its hating of the self life and its entire denial of self, with its growing conformity to the crucified Redeemer in His deep humility and entire surrender of His will to the life of God. To have such a mind requires us to be one with *Christ* in His inward parts.

CHRIST IN ME

"I have been crucified with *Christ*; it is no longer I who live, but *Christ* lives in me; and the life which I now live in the flesh I live by faith in the Son of God, who loved me and gave Himself for me." (Galatians 2:20)

The thought of fellowship with *Christ* in His bearing the cross has often led to the vain attempt in our own power to follow Him and bear His image. But this is impossible to man until he first learns to know what it means to say, "I have been crucified with *Christ*."

When Adam died, all his descendants died with him and in him. In his sin in paradise, and in the spiritual death into which he fell, I had a share: I died in him. And the power of that sin and death, in which all his descendants share, works in every child of Adam every day.

Christ came as the second Adam. In His death on the cross all who believe in Him had a share. Each one may say in truth, "I have been crucified with *Christ*." As the representative of His people, He took them up with Him on the cross, and me too. The life that He gives is the crucified life, in which He entered heaven and was exalted to the throne, standing as a Lamb as it had been slain. The power of His death and life work in me, and as I hold fast the truth that I have been crucified with Him, and now I myself live no more, but *Christ* lives in me, I receive power to conquer sin; the life that I have received from Him is a life that has been crucified and made free from the power of sin.

We have a deep and very precious truth. Some Christians have little knowledge of it. That knowledge is not gained easily. It needs a great longing in very deed to be dead to all sin. It needs a strong faith, brought by the Holy Spirit, that the union with *Christ* crucified [the fellowship of His cross] can day by day become our life.

The life that He lives in heaven has its strength and its glory in the fact that it is a crucified life. And the life that He imparts to the believer is a crucified life with its victory over sin and its power of access into God's presence.

It is in very true that I no longer live, but *Christ* lives in me as a Crucified One. As *faith* realizes and holds fast the fact that the crucified *Christ* lives in me, life in the fellowship of the cross becomes a possibility and a blessed experience.

CRUCIFY THE WORLD

"But God forbid that I should boast except in the cross of our Lord Jesus *Christ,* by whom [the cross] the world has been crucified to me, and I to the world." (Galatians 6:14)

What Paul had written in Galatians in the end of the letter speaks strongly of his only glory being that in *Christ* he has in very deed been crucified to the world and entirely delivered from its power. When he said "I have been crucified with *Christ*," it was not only an inner spiritual truth, but an actual practical experience in relation to the world and its temptations.

Christ had spoken about the world hating Him, and He overcoming the world. Paul knows that the world, which nailed *Christ* to the cross, had in that deed done the same to him. He boasts that he lives as one crucified to the world, and now the world as an impotent [lacking power] enemy was crucified to him. It was this that made him glory in the cross of *Christ*. It had brought out a complete deliverance from the world.

How very different the relation of Christians to the world in our day. They agree that they may not commit the sins that the world allows. But except for they are good friends with the world, and have liberty to enjoy as much of it as they can, if they only keep from open sin. They do not know the most dangerous source of sin: is the love of the world.

When the world crucified *Christ*, it crucified you with Him, When *Christ* overcame the world on the cross, He made you an over comer too. He calls you now, at whatever cost of self-denial, to regard the world, in its hostility to God and His kingdom, as a crucified enemy who by the cross is a winner. Amen!

What a different relationship to the pleasures and attractions of the world the Christian, by the Holy Spirit, has learned to say: "I have been crucified with *Christ*; the crucified *Christ* lives in me"! Let us pray to God passionately that the Holy Spirit, through whom *Christ* offered Himself on the cross, may reveal to us in power what it means to "glory to the cross of our Lord Jesus Christ, through which the world had been crucified to me."

IN MY FLESH

"And those who are *Christ's* have crucified the flesh with its passions and desires." (Galatians 5:24)

Paul in reference of the flesh says (Romans 7:18), "For I know that in me [that is, in my flesh] nothing good dwells; for to will is present with me, but how to perform what is good I do not find.." And again (Romans 8:7), "Because the carnal mind is enmity against God; for it is not subject to the law of God, nor indeed can be." When Adam lost the spirit of God, he became flesh. Flesh is the expression for the evil, corrupt nature that we inherit from Adam. Of this flesh it is written, "knowing this, that our old man was crucified with Him, that the body of sin might be done away with, that we should no longer be slaves of sin" (Romans 6:6). And Paul puts it here even more strongly, "They that are in *Christ Jesus* have crucified the flesh."

When the disciples heard and obeyed the call of Jesus to follow Him, they honestly meant to do so, but as He explained what that would imply, they were far from being ready to yield. And even those who are *Christ's* and have accepted Him as the Crucified One - few understand what that includes. By that act of surrender they actually have crucified the flesh and consented to regard it as an accursed thing, nailed to the cross of *Christ*.

It may be that the preaching of *Christ* crucified has been defective or the truth of our being crucified with *Christ* has not been taught. They shrink back from the self-denial that it implies, and as a result, where the flesh is allowed in any measure to have its way, the Spirit of *Christ* cannot exert His power.

Paul taught the Galatians: "Walk in the Spirit, and you shall not fulfill the lust of the flesh." "For as many as are led by the Spirit of God, these are sons of God." And only as the flesh is kept in the place of crucifixion can the Spirit guide us in living faith and fellowship with *Christ Jesus*.

It is the life of the soul that has been counted as hopeless by God and has been put on the cross and crucified with *Christ*. The old man was the life of the soul, but now, since the old man has been crucified, our soul *should* act only as an organ of *Christ* and *should* be under control of our spirit, having *Christ* as its life.

Christ lives in you, the Crucified One, and now you may forever glory in the cross on which the world and the flesh are crucified.

TAKE YOUR CROSS

"And he who does not take his cross and follow after Me is not worthy of Me. He who finds his life will lose it, and he who loses his life for My sake will find it." (Matthew 10:38-39)

We will find that what Paul could teach openly and fully after the crucifixion, was given by the Master in words that could at first hardly be understood, and yet contained the *seed* of the full truth.

It was in the ordination charge, when *Christ* sent forth His disciples, that He first used the expression that the disciple must take up his cross and follow Him.

The only meaning the disciples could attach to these words was what they had often seen, when an evil-doer who had been sentenced to death by the cross was led out bearing his cross to the place of execution. In bearing the cross, he acknowledged the sentence of death that was on him. And *Christ* would have His disciples understand that their nature was so evil and corrupt that it was only in losing their natural life that they could find the true life. Of Himself it was true that all His life He bore His cross - the sentence of death that He knew to rest upon Himself on account of our sins. And so He would have each disciple bear his cross - the sentence of death upon himself and his evil, carnal nature.

The disciples could not at once understand all this. But *Christ* gave them seed words, which would germinate in their hearts and later on begin to reveal their full meaning. The disciple was not only to carry the sentence of death in himself, but to learn that in following the Master to His cross he would find the power to lose his life and to receive the life that would come through the cross of *Christ*.

Christ asks of His disciples that they should forsake all and take up their cross, give up their whole will and life, and follow Him. To take the will of God by putting themselves aside. This demand requested of that they at any cost first give their love to Him that they might be worthy of Him.

He who loses his life for His sake will find it. In other words to find the soul-life is to allow the soul to have its enjoyment and to escape suffering. To lose the soul-life is to cause the soul to lose its enjoyment and suffer. If the followers of *Christ* allow their soul to have its enjoyment in this age, they will cause their soul to suffer the loss of enjoyment in the coming kingdom age. But if they allow their soul to suffer the loss of enjoyment in this age then they *will* enable their soul to have enjoyment in the coming kingdom age and share the King's ruling over earth.

The call comes to us too to give up the self life with its self-enjoyment, and bear the cross in fellowship with Him - and we will share in His victory!

"Now to him that is able to keep you from falling, and to present you faultless before the presence of his glory with exceeding joy." (Jude 1:24)

DENY SELF

Then Jesus said to His disciples, "If anyone desires to come after Me, let him deny himself, and take up his cross, and follow Me." (Matthew 16:24)

Christ had for the first time definitely announced that He would have to suffer much and be killed and be raised again. "Peter rebuked Him, saying, '"Far be it from You, Lord; this shall not happen to You!'" *Christ's* answer was, "Get behind Me, Satan."

The spirit of Peter, seeking to turn Him away from the cross and its suffering, was nothing but Satan tempting Him to turn aside from the path which God had appointed as our way of salvation. *Christ* perceived that it was not Peter but Satan who was frustrating Him from taken the cross. This reveals that our natural man can not carry the cross and is one with Satan.

Christ then adds the words of our text, in which He uses for the second time the words "take up the cross." But with that He reveals what is implied in the cross: "If any man come after Me, let him deny himself, and take up his cross." When Adam sinned, he fell from eternal life with

God out of heaven, and into the life of the self-world. Self then became the law of his life.

When Jesus *Christ* came to restore man to his original place, "being in the form of God, He emptied Himself, taking the form of a servant, and humbled Himself even to the death of the cross." What He has done Himself He asks of all who desire to follow Him: "If anyone desires to come after Me, let him deny himself."

Instead of denying himself, Peter denied his Lord: "I know not the man." The secret of true discipleship is to bear the cross, to acknowledge the death sentence that has been passed on self, and to deny any right that self has to rule over us. The surrender to *Christ* is to: not allow the self to come down from the cross to which it has been crucified.

When we are setting our minds on the things of men, we become Satan., a stumbling block to the Lord on His way to fulfill God's plan.

In this chapter we learn that three terms are related to one another: mind, himself, and soul-life. You set your mind on God, deny self, and lose your soul-life [to find it].

Our mind is the expression of our self, and our self is the embodiment of our soul-life. Our soul-life is embodied in and lived out by our self, and our self is expressed through our mind, our thought, our concept, our opinion.

When we set our mind on the things of men, our mind acts and expresses it-self. This was what happened to Peter. He had to deny himself, not save his soul-life but lose it. To take up the cross is by losing the soul-life [denying self].

As His believers we now bear the cross.

HIS DISCIPLE

"If any man comes to Me, and hate not his own life, he cannot be My disciple. And whoever does not bear his cross and come after Me cannot be My disciple. whoever of you does not forsake all that he has cannot be My disciple." (Luke 14:26-33)

For the third time *Christ* speaks about bearing the cross. He gives new meaning to it when He says that a man must hate his own life and renounce all he has. Three times over He repeats the words that without this a man *cannot* be His disciple.

"If a man hate not his own life." And why does *Christ* make such an strict demand the condition of discipleship? Because the sinful nature we have inherited from Adam is indeed so vile and full of sin that, if our eyes were only opened to see it in its true nature, we would flee from it as hideous evil. "The flesh is hostile against God"; the soul that seeks to love God cannot but hate the "old man" which is corrupt through its whole being. Nothing less than this, the hating of our own life, will make us willing to bear the cross and carry within us the sentence of death on our evil nature. It is not until we hate this life with a deadly hatred that we will be ready to give up the old nature to die the death that is its due.

Christ has one more word: "He that doesn't disown all that he has," whether in property or character, "cannot be My disciple." *Christ* claims all!

Christ undertakes to satisfy every need and to give a hundredfold more than we give up. It is when by faith we become conscious what it means to know *Christ*, and to love Him and to receive from Him what can in very deed enrich and satisfy our immortal spirits, that we shall count the surrender of what at first appeared so difficult, our highest privilege.

As we learn what it means that *Christ* is our life, we should account (all things) but loss, for the excellency of the knowledge of *Christ* Jesus our Lord. In the path of following Him, and in continual learning to know and to love Him better, we willingly sacrifice all, our-self with its life, to make room for Him who is *more* than all.

LETS GO

Then Jesus, looking at him, loved him, and said to him, "One thing you lack: Go your way, sell whatever you have and give to the poor, and you will have treasure in heaven; and come, take up the cross, and follow Me." (Mark 10:21)

When *Christ* spoke these words to the young ruler, he went away grieved. Jesus said: "How hardly shall they that have riches enter into the kingdom of God!" The disciples were astonished at His words. When *Christ* repeated once again what He had said, they were astonished out of measure, "Who then can be saved? "Jesus looking upon them said, "With men it is impossible, but not with God; for with God all things are possible."

Christ had spoken about bearing the cross from the human side, as the one condition of discipleship. Here with the rich young ruler He reveals from the side of God what is needed to give men the will and the power to sacrifice all, if they are to enter the kingdom. He said to Peter, when he had confessed Him as *Christ*, the Son of God, that flesh and blood had not revealed it to him, but His Father in heaven, to remind him and the other disciples that it was only by divine teaching that he could make the confession. So here with the ruler He unveils the great mystery that it is only by *divine* power that a man can take up his cross, can lose his life, can deny himself and hate the life to which he is attached by nature.

What multitudes have seek to follow *Christ* and obey His order [command] - and have found that they have utterly failed. What multitudes have felt that *Christ's* claims were beyond their reach and have chose to be Christians without any attempt at the whole-hearted devotion and the entire self-denial which *Christ* asks for!

Let us in our study of what the fellowship of the cross means and take today's message to heart and believe that it is only by putting our trust in the living God, and in the mighty power with which He is willing to work in the heart, that we can attempt to be disciples who forsake all and follow *Christ* in the fellowship of His cross.

A GRAIN

"Most assuredly, I say to you, unless a grain of wheat falls into the ground and dies, it remains alone; but if it dies, it produces much grain. He who loves his life will lose it, and he who hates his life in this world will keep it for eternal life." (John 12:24-25)

All nature is a parable of how the losing of a life can be the way of securing a truer and higher life. Every grain of wheat, every seed throughout the world, teaches the lesson that through death lies the path to beautiful and fruitful life.

It was so with the Son of God. He had to pass through death in all its bitterness and suffering before He could rise to heaven and impart His life to His redeemed people. And here under the shadow of the approaching cross He calls His disciples: "If any man will serve Me, let him follow Me." He repeats the words: "He that hates his life in this world shall keep it for eternal life."

One might have thought that *Christ* did not need to lose His holy life. But so it was: God had laid upon Him the sins of the whole world, and He yielded to the relentless law: Through death to life and to fruit.

How should we, in the consciousness of that evil nature and that death which we inherited in Adam, be grateful that there is a way open to us, in the fellowship of *Christ* and His cross, we can die to this accursed self! With what willingness and gratitude should we listen to the call to bear our cross, to yield our 'old man' as crucified with *Christ* daily to that death which he deserves!

Surely the thought that the power of the eternal Life is working in us, should make us willing and glad to die the death that brings us into the fellowship and the power of life in a risen *Christ*.

We have seen and believe what is impossible to man is possible to God. Let us believe that the law of the Spirit of *Christ* Jesus, the risen Lord, can in very deed make His death and His life the daily experience of our souls.

HIS WILL

He went a little farther and fell on His face, and prayed, saying, "O My Father, if it is possible, let this cup pass from Me; nevertheless, not as I will, but as You will." (Matthew 26:39)

The death of *Christ* on the cross is the highest and the holiest that can be known of Him even in the glory of heaven. And the highest and the holiest that the Holy Spirit can work in us is to take us up and to keep us in the fellowship of the cross of *Christ*. We need to enter deeply into the truth that *Christ* the beloved Son of the Father could not return to the glory of heaven until He had first given Himself over unto death. As this great truth opens up to us it will help us to understand how in our life, and in our fellowship with *Christ*, it is impossible for us to share His life until we have first in very deed surrendered ourselves every day to die to sin and the world, and so to abide in the unbroken fellowship with our crucified Lord.

And it is from *Christ* alone that we can learn what it means to have fellowship with His sufferings, and to be made conformable unto His death. When in the agony of Gethsemane He looked forward to what a death on the cross would be, He got such a vision of what it meant to die the accursed death under the power of sin - with God's countenance so turned from Him that not a single ray of its light could penetrate the darkness - that He prayed the cup might pass from Him. But when no answer came, and He understood that the Father could not allow the cup to pass by, He yielded up His whole will and life in the word: "Thy will be done." In this word of our Lord in agony, you can enter into fellowship with Him; in His strength your heart will be made strong to believe that God in His omnipotence will enable you in very deed with *Christ* to yield up everything, because you have in very deed been crucified with Him.

"YOUR will be done" - let this be the deepest and the highest word in your life. In the power of *Christ* with whom you have been crucified, and in the power of His Spirit, the definite daily surrender to the ever-blessed will of God will become the joy and the strength of your life.

WE ARE LOVED

Then Jesus said, "Father, forgive them, for they do not know what they do." (Luke 23:34)

The seven words on the cross reveal what the mind of *Christ* is, and show the dispositions that become His disciples. Take the three first words, all the expression of His wonderful love.

"Father, forgive them, for they do not what they do." He prays for His enemies. In the hour of their triumph over Him, and of the shame and suffering which they delight in showering on Him, He pours out His love in prayer for them. It is the call to everyone who believes in a crucified *Christ* to go and do likewise, even as He has said, "Love your enemies, bless them that curse you, do good to them that hate you, and pray for them which persecute you."

The law of the Master is the law for the disciple; the love of the crucified Jesus, the only *rule* for those who believe in Him.

"Woman, behold your son!" "Behold your mother!" The love that cared for His enemies cared too for His friends. Jesus felt what the anguish must be in the heart of His widowed mother, and commits her to the care of the beloved disciple. He knew that for John there could be no higher privilege, and no more blessed service, than that of taking His place in the care of Mary. Even so, we who are the disciples of *Christ* must not only pray for His enemies, but prove our love to Him and to all who belong to Him by seeing to it that every solitary one is comforted, and that every loving heart has some work to do in caring for those who belong to the blessed Master.

"Assuredly, I say to you, today you will be with Me in Paradise." The penitent thief had appealed to *Christ's* mercy to remember him. With willingness of joy and **'love'** *Christ* gives the immediate answer to his prayer! Whether it was the love that prays for His enemies, or the love that cares for His friends, or the love that rejoices over the penitent sinner who was being cast out by man - in all *Christ* proves that the cross is a cross of love, that the Crucified One is the embodiment of a love that passes knowledge.

With every thought of what we owe to that love, with every act of faith in which we rejoice in its redemption, let us prove that the mind of the crucified *Christ* is our mind, and that His love is not only what we trust for ourselves, but what guides us in our loving relation with the world around us.

SACRIFICE MADE

"My God, My God, why have You forsaken Me?" - "I thirst." - "It is finished." (Matthew 27:46, John 19:28,30)

The first three words on the cross reveal love in its outflow to men. The next three reveal love in the tremendous sacrifice that it brought, necessary to deliver us from our sins and give the victory over every enemy. They still reveal the very mind that was in *Christ*, and that is to be the very nature of our whole life.

"My God, My God, why have You forsaken Me?" How deep the darkness must of been that overshadowed Him, for not one ray of light could pierce, and He could not say "My Father"! It was this awful desertion breaking in upon that life of childlike fellowship with the Father, in which He had always walked, that caused Him the agony and the bloody sweat in Gethsemane. "O My Father, let this cup pass from Me" - but it might not be, and He bowed His head in submission: "Your will be done." It was His love to God and love to man - this yielding Himself to the very uttermost. As we learn to believe and to worship that love, then we too will learn to say: "My Father, Your will be done."

"I thirst." The body now gives expression to the terrible experience of what it passed through when the fire of God's wrath against sin came upon *Christ* in the hour of His desertion. He had spoken of Dives crying (rich man) "I am tormented in this flame." *Christ* utters His complaint of what He was suffering.

Studies show that in crucifixion the whole body is in agony with a terrible fever and pain. Our Lord endured it all and cried: "I thirst"; soul and body was the sacrifice He brought to the Father. The glorious truth of thirst on the cross is that we don't need to be thirsty; our thirst for God can be quenched because Jesus was thirsty for us.

And then comes the great word: "It is finished." All that there was to suffer and endure had been brought as a willing sacrifice; He had finished the work the Father gave Him to do. His love held nothing back. He gave Himself an offering and a sacrifice.

Such was the mind of *Christ*, and such must be the disposition of everyone who owes himself and his life to that sacrifice. The mind that was in *Christ* must be in us, ready to say: "I have come to do the will of Him who sent Me, and to finish His work." And every day that our confidence grows fuller in *Christ's* finished work, we then see our heart more entirely yielding itself like Him, in the goal of being Christ-like, while in the service of God and His love.

DEATH IN CHRIST

And when Jesus had cried out with a loud voice, He said, "Father, 'into Your hands I commit My spirit.'" Having said this, He breathed His last. (Luke 23:46)

Like David (Psalm 31:5), *Christ* had often committed His spirit into the hands of His Father for His daily life and need. But here is something new and very special. He gives up His spirit into the power of death, gives up all control over it, to sink down into the darkness and death of the grave, where He can neither think, nor pray, nor will. He surrenders Himself into the Father's hands, *trusting* Him to care for Him in the dark, and in due time to raise Him up again.

If we have truly died in *Christ*, and are now in faith every day to carry with us the death of our Lord Jesus, this word is the very one that we need. Just think once again what *Christ* meant when He said that we must hate and lose our life. We died in Adam; the life we receive from him is death; there is nothing good or heavenly in us by nature. It is to this inward evil nature, to all the life that we have from this world, that we must die. There cannot be any thought of any real holiness without totally dying to this self, our old man.

Many deceive themselves because they seek to be alive in God before they are dead to their own nature - a thing as impossible as it is for a grain of wheat to be alive before it dies. This total dying to self lies at the root of all true piety. The spiritual life must *grow* out of death.

And if we ask how we can do this, we find the answer in the mind in which *Christ* died. Like Him we cast ourselves upon God, without knowing how the new life is to be attained; but as we in fellowship with Jesus say, "Father, into Your hands I commit my spirit," and depend absolutely upon God to raise us up into the new life, there will be 'fulfilled' in us the wonderful promise of God's Word concerning the exceeding greatness of His power in us who believe, according to the mighty power which He bestowed in *Christ* when He raised Him from the dead.

This indeed is the true test of faith - a faith that lives every day and every hour in absolute dependence upon the continual and immediate quickening of the *divine* life in us by God Himself through the Holy Spirit. We have died in Christ through His death, but now He lives in us through His resurrection.

FINISH HIS WORK

So when Jesus had received the sour wine, He said, "It is finished!" And bowing His head, He gave up His spirit. (John 19:30)

The seven words of our Lord on the cross reveal to us His mind and disposition. At the beginning of His ministry He said (John 4:34): Jesus said to them, "My food is to do the will of Him who sent Me, and to finish His work." In all things, the small as well as the great, He should accomplish God's work. In the High Priestly Prayer at the end of the three years' ministry He could say (John 17:4): "I have glorified You on the earth. I have finished the work which You have given Me to do." He sacrificed all, and in dying on the cross could in truth say: "It is finished."

With that word to the Father He laid down His life. With that word He was strengthened, after the terrible agony on the cross, in the knowledge that all was now fulfilled. And with that word He uttered the truth of the gospel of our redemption, that all that was needed for man's salvation had been accomplished on the cross!

This disposition should characterize every follower of *Christ*. The mind that was in Him must be in us - it must be our meat, the strength of our life, to do the will of God in all things, and, to finish His work. There may be small things about which we are not conscientious, and so we bring harm to ourselves and to God's work. Or we draw back before some great thing which demands too much sacrifice. In every case we may find strength to perform our duty in *Christ's* word "It is finished."

His finished work secured the victory over every foe. By faith we may appropriate that dying word of *Christ* on the cross, and find the power for daily living and dying in the fellowship of the crucified *Christ*.

Please study the *treasure* contained in this word: "It is finished." Faith in what *Christ* accomplished on the cross will enable you to manifest in daily life the spirit of the cross.

What was it that Jesus finished? Jesus paid the full penalty for my sins and yours. 'Paid in full' is the equivalent phrase in the Greek language. His most precious blood flowed freely on that Historic occasion.

Jesus paid my sin debt by dying on the tree.

DIED TO SIN

"Certainly not! How shall we who died to sin live any longer in it?" (Romans 6:2)

After having, in the first section of the Epistle to the Romans (1:16 to 5:11), expounded the great doctrine of justification by faith, Paul proceeds, in the second section (5:12 to 8:39), to unfold the related doctrine of the new life by faith in *Christ*. Taking Adam as a figure of *Christ*, he teaches that just as we all really and actually died in Adam, so that his death reigns in our nature, even so, in *Christ*, those who believe in Him adequately died to sin, were set free from it, and became partakers of the new holy life of *Christ*.

He asks the question: "How shall we who died to sin live any longer in it?" In these words we have the deep spiritual truth that our death to sin in *Christ* delivers us from its power, so that we no longer may or need to live in it. The secret of true and full holiness is by faith, and in the power of the Holy Spirit, to live in the consciousness: I am dead to sin. In explaining this truth he reminds them that they were baptized into the death of *Christ*. We were buried with Him through baptism into death. We became united with Him by the likeness of His death. Our 'old man' was crucified with Him, that the body of sin might be done away - rendered void and powerless.

Take time and quietly, asking for the teaching of the Holy Spirit, ponder these words until the truth masters you: I am *dead* to sin in *Christ* Jesus. As we grow in the consciousness of our union with the crucified *Christ*, we shall experience that the power of His life in us has made us free from the power of sin.

In Romans 6 Jesus teaches us that our 'old man', the 'old nature' that is in us, was actually crucified with Him, so now we are no longer in bondage to sin. But remember it is only as the Holy Spirit makes *Christ's* death a reality within us that we will know, not by force of argument or conviction, but in the reality of the power of a divine life, that we are in very deed dead to sin. It only needs a continual living in *Christ J*esus.

GET RIGHT

For what does the Scripture say? "Abraham believed God, and it was accounted to him for righteousness" in the presence of Him whom he believed - God, who gives life to the dead and calls those things which do not exist as though they did." (Romans 4:3,7)

Now, after listening to the words of our Lord Jesus about our fellowship with Him in the cross, turn to Paul, and see how through the Holy Spirit he gives the deeper insight into what our death in *Christ* means.

You know how the first section of Romans is devoted to the doctrine of justification by faith in *Christ*. After speaking (1:18-32) of the awful sin of the heathen, and then (2:1-29) of the sin of the Jew, he points out how Jew and Gentile are "guilty before God," "All have sinned and come short." And then he states that the free grace which gave the redemption is in *Christ* Jesus (3:21-31). In chapter 4 he points to Abraham as having, [when he believed], understood that God justified him freely by His grace, and not for *anything* he had done.

Abraham not only believed this, but something more. "He believed in God, who gives life to the dead, and calls those things which do not exist as though they did."

The two expressions are most significant, as indicating the two essential needs there are in the redemption of man in *Christ* Jesus. There is the need of justification by faith, to restore man to the favor of God. But there is more needed. He must also be quickened to a new life. Just as justification is by faith alone, so is regeneration. *Christ* died on account of our sins; He was raised again on account of our justification.

In the first section (down to chap. 5:11) Paul deals solely with the great thought of our justification. But in the second section (5:12 to 8:39) he explains that wonderful union with *Christ,* through faith, by which we died with Him, by which we *live* in Him, and by which, through the Holy Spirit, we are made free, not only from the punishment, but also from the power of sin, and are enabled to live the life of righteousness, of obedience, and of sanctification.

LIFE WITH CHRIST

"Now if we died with *Christ,* we believe that we shall also live with Him." (Romans 6:8)

We need to understand in the power of the resurrection life of *Christ.* By understanding we are transcendent over corruption and death since we are one with Him in resurrection. How clearly this appears from what Paul says: "Now if we died with *Christ,* we believe that we shall also live with Him"; it is the knowledge and experience that gives us the assurance of the power of His resurrection in us. "For the death that He died, He died to sin once for all; but the life that He lives, He lives to God." It is only because we know that we are dead with Him, that we can live with Him. (verse 10)

On the strength of this, Paul now appeals to his readers. "Likewise you also, reckon yourselves to be dead indeed to sin, but alive to God in *Christ* Jesus our Lord." (verse 11) The words "even so reckon yourselves" are a call to an act of bold and confident faith. Reckon yourselves to be indeed dead unto sin, as much as Christ is, and alive to God in Christ Jesus.

The word gives us a divine assurance of what we actually are and have in *Christ.* And this is a truth that our minds can master and appropriate, but a reality which the Holy Spirit will reveal within us. In His power we accept our death with *Christ* on the cross as the power of our daily life.

Then we are able to accept and obey the command: "Therefore do not let sin reign in your mortal body, that you should obey it in its lusts. And do not present your members as instruments of unrighteousness to sin, but present yourselves to God as being alive from the dead, and your members as instruments of righteousness to God. For sin shall not have dominion over you, for you are not under law but under grace" (verse 12-14). "And having been set free from sin, you became slaves of righteousness."I speak in human terms because of the weakness of your flesh. For just as you presented your members as slaves of uncleanness, and of lawlessness leading to more lawlessness, so now present your members as slaves of righteousness for holiness. But now having been set free from sin, and having become slaves of God, you have your fruit to holiness, and the end, everlasting life. (verse 18,19,22).

The whole chapter is a wonderful revelation of the deep meaning of its opening words: "How shall we who died to sin live any longer in it?" Everything depends upon our acceptance of the divine assurance: If we died with *Christ*, as He died, and now lives to God, we too have the assurance that in Him we have the power to live unto God.

THE LAW

"Therefore, my brethren, you also have become dead to the law through the body of *Christ*, that you may be married to another to Him who was raised from the dead, that we should bear fruit to God." "But now we have been delivered from the law, having died to what we were held by, so that we should serve in the newness of the Spirit and not in the oldness of the letter." (Romans 7:4,6)

The believer is not only dead to sin, but dead to the law. This is a deeper truth, giving us deliverance from the thought of a life of effort and failure, and opening the way to the life in the power of the Holy Spirit. "Thou shalt" is done away with; the *power* of the Spirit takes its place. In the remainder of this chapter (7:7-24) we have a description of the Christian as he still tries to obey the law, but utterly fails. He experiences that "in him, that in his flesh, dwells no good thing." He finds that the law of sin continually brings him into captivity, and compels the cry: "O wretched man that I am! Who will deliver me from this body of death?"

In the whole passage, it is everywhere "I," without any thought of the Spirit's help. It is only when he has given utterance to his cry of despair that he is brought to see that he is no longer under the law, but under the rule of the

Holy Spirit (8:1,2). "There is now no condemnation," such as he had experienced in his attempt to obey the law, "For the law of the Spirit of life in *Christ* Jesus has made me free from the law of sin and death."

As Romans 7 gives us the experience that leads to being a captive under the power of sin, Romans 8 reveals the experience of the life of a man in *Christ* Jesus, who has now been made free from the law of sin and death. In the former we have the life of the ordinary Christian doing his own will to keep the commandments of the law, and to walk in His ways, but realizing the failure and shortcomings.

In the latter we have the man who knows that he is in *Christ* Jesus, dead to sin and alive to God, and by the Spirit has been made free and is kept free from the bondage of sin and of death.

A deeper study of Romans 7 shows that a man learns that in him, that is in his flesh, there is "no" good thing, and there is no deliverance from this state but to yield to the power of the Spirit making him free from the power and bondage of the flesh, and so fulfilling the righteousness of the law in the power of the life of *Christ*!

This chapter is primarily about the flesh [mind and soul] trying to please God with the good of the natural life. Although this is the situation of an unsaved person, most

Christians still pass through this type of experience even after being saved. Also just a note here: the tenth commandment, "You shall not covet," isn't related to outward conduct, but rather the sin that indwells within him [thoughts].

CONDEMN THE FLESH

"For what the law could not do in that it was weak through the flesh, God did by sending His own Son in the likeness of sinful flesh, on account of sin: He condemned sin in the flesh." (Romans 8:3)

In Romans 8:7 Paul writes: "Because the carnal mind is enmity against God; for it is not subject to the law of God, nor indeed can be." Paul opens up the depth of sin that is in the flesh. In chapter 7 he said 'that in the flesh there is no good thing.' Here he goes deeper, and tells us that it is hostile against God: it hates God and His law. It was on this account that God condemned sin in the flesh on the cross; all the curse that is sin is in the flesh in which sin dwells. The believer needs to understand to cease from any attempt in 'seeking' to be perfect in the flesh what has begun in the Spirit. The two are at deadly, hostile to each other.

See how this lies at the very root of the true Christian life (verse 8:3,4): "God *condemned* sin in the flesh, that the righteousness of the law might be fulfilled in us who walk, not after the flesh, but after the Spirit." All the requirements of God's law will be fulfilled, not in those who strive to keep and fulfill that law, but in those who walk by the Spirit, and in His power live out the life that *Christ* won for us on the cross and imparted to us in the resurrection.

In me, that is in my flesh, in the old nature which I have from Adam, there dwells literally no good thing that can satisfy the eye of a holy God. And that flesh can *never* by any process of discipline, or struggling, or prayer, be made better than it is. But the Son of God in the likeness of sinful flesh - in the form of a man - condemned sin on the cross. "There is therefore now no condemnation to those who are in *Christ* Jesus, who do not walk according to the flesh, but according to the Spirit." (verse 8:1)

The flesh is of sin, yet the Son of God became flesh. He was in the *likeness* of the flesh and did not have the sin of the flesh. He was crucified in the flesh. On the cross He judged Satan who is related to the flesh, and the world, which hangs on him thereby destroying Satan. At this time God condemned sin, which was brought by Satan into man's flesh.

As a result it is now possible for us to walk [not by the flesh] but by the Spirit so the righteous requirement of the law might be fulfilled in us.

CHRIST CRUCIFIED

"For I determined not to know anything among you except Jesus *Christ* and Him crucified. And my speech and my preaching were not with persuasive words of human wisdom, but in demonstration of the Spirit and of power." (1 Corinthians 2:2,4)

This text is Paul's purpose in his preaching: to know nothing but Jesus *Christ* and Him crucified. But it contains a far deeper thought. He speaks of his purpose, not only in the matter of his preaching, but in his whole spirit and life to prove how he [in everything] seeks to act in conformity to the crucified *Christ*. Then he writes (2 Corinthians 13:4): "For though He was crucified in weakness, yet He lives by the power of God. For we also are weak in Him, but we shall live with Him by the power of God toward you." Examine yourselves as to whether you are in the faith. Do you not know that Jesus *Christ* is in you? His whole ministry and manner of life bore the mark of *Christ's* likeness - crucified through weakness, yet living by the power of God.

Just before the words of our text Paul had written in (1 Cor.1:17-24): "For the message of the cross is foolishness to those who are perishing, but to us who are being saved it is the power of God " It was not only in his preaching, but in his whole disposition and behavior that he seeks to act in harmony with that weakness in which *Christ* was crucified. He had identified himself with the weakness of the cross, and its shame, that in his whole life and conduct he would prove that in everything he searched and then showed the likeness and the spirit of the crucified Jesus. Then he says (verse 2:3): "I was with you in weakness, in fear, and in much trembling."

It is on this account that he spoke so strongly: "For *Christ* did not send me to baptize, but to preach the gospel, not with wisdom of words, lest the cross of *Christ* should be made of no effect." (verse 1:17); "And my speech and my preaching were not with persuasive words of human wisdom, but in demonstration of the Spirit and of power" (verse 2:4). Is this not the great reason why the power of God is so little manifested in the preaching of the gospel? *Christ* the crucified may be the subject of the preaching and yet there may be such confidence in human learning and eloquence that there is nothing to be seen of that likeness of the crucified Jesus which alone gives preaching its supernatural, its divine power.

Every believer *must* bear the hallmark, the stamp of the sanctuary. Nothing but Jesus *Christ*, and Him crucified.

SELF-RESTRAINT

"And everyone who competes for the prize is temperate in all things. Now they do it to obtain a perishable crown, but we for an imperishable crown." "But I discipline my body and bring it into subjection." (1 Corinthians 9:25, 27)

Paul reminds us of the well-known principle that anyone competing for a prize in the public games is "temperate in all things." Everything, however attractive, that might be a hindrance in the race is given up or set aside. And this in order to obtain an earthly prize. And should we, who *strive* for an incorruptible crown, and that *Christ* may be Lord of all - should we not be self-restraint in all things that could in the very least prevent our following the Lord Jesus with an undivided heart?

Paul says: "But I discipline my body and bring it into subjection." He allowed nothing to hinder him. He tells us: "This one thing I do: I press towards the *mark* for the prize." No self-pleasing in eating and drinking, no comfort or ease, should for a moment keep him from showing the spirit of the cross in his daily life, or from sacrificing all, like his Master. Read the following four passages which comprise his life-history: 1 Corinthians 4:11-13; 2 Corinthians 4:8-12, 6:4-10, 11:23-27.

The cross was not only the theme of his preaching, but the *rule* of his life in all its details.

Let us pray that this disposition may be found in all Christians and preachers of the gospel, through the power of the Holy Spirit. When the death of *Christ* works with power in the preacher, then *Christ's* life will be known among the people. Let us pray that the fellowship of the cross may regain its old place, and that God's children may obey the injunction: "Let this mind be in you that was in *Christ* Jesus." For if we have been united together in the likeness of His death, certainly we will also be in the likeness of His resurrection." (Romans 6:5)

Did you know that there is a reward? Yes, we His believers, have all received His salvation through faith in Him. This has been settled once and for all. To be rewarded by Him will depend on how we run the race. (2 Tim. 4:6-8)

CARRY THE BODY

"Always carrying about in the body the dying of the Lord Jesus, that the life of Jesus also may be manifested in our body." "So then death is working in us, but life in you." (2 Corinthians 4:10,12)

Paul is very bold in speaking of the intimate union that there was between *Christ* living in him and the life he lived in the flesh, with all its suffering. He had spoken (Galatians 2:20) of his being crucified with *Christ*, and *Christ* living in him. He tells how he was always bearing about [in his body] the dying of Jesus; it was through this that the life of Jesus manifested in his body. And he says that it was because of the death of *Christ* that was working in and through him that *Christ's* life could work in them.

We often speak of our abiding in *Christ*. But we forget that this means the abiding in a crucified *Christ*. Many believers appear to think that when once they have claimed *Christ's* death in the fellowship of the cross, and have counted themselves as crucified with Him, that they may now consider it a done thing. They do not understand that *it is* in the crucified *Christ*, and in the fellowship of His death, that they are to abide daily and endlessly. The fellowship of the cross is to be the *life* of a daily experience, the self-emptying of our Lord, His taking the form of a servant, His humbling Himself and becoming obedient until death, even the death of the cross - this mind that was in *Christ* is to be the disposition that marks our daily life.

"Always carrying about in the body the dying of Jesus." As Paul this is what we are called to as well. If we are to live for the welfare of men around us, if we are to sacrifice our ease and pleasure to win souls for our Lord, it must be true of us, [as Paul], that we are able to say: Death works in us, but life in those for who we pray and labor. For it is in the fellowship of the sufferings of *Christ* that the crucified Lord can live out and work out His life in us and through us.

We learn that the abiding in *Christ* Jesus is nothing less than the abiding of the Crucified in us, and we in Him.

This putting to death of Jesus consumes our natural man, our outward man, our flesh, so that our inward man may have the opportunity to develop and be renewed. "For we who live are always delivered to death for Jesus' sake, that the life of Jesus also may be manifested in our mortal flesh." (2 Corinthians 4:11)

THE SPIRIT LEADS

"How much more shall the blood of *Christ*, who through the eternal Spirit offered Himself without spot to God, cleanse your conscience from dead works to serve the living God?" (Hebrews 9:14)

The cross is *Christ's* highest glory. The glory which He received from the Father was entirely due to His humbling of Himself to the death of the cross. "Therefore God also has highly exalted Him and given Him the name which is above every name." (Philippians 2:9). The greatest work which the Holy Spirit could ever do in the Son of God was when He enabled Him to yield Himself a sacrifice and an offering for a sweet-smelling aroma [savior] (Ephesians 5:2). And the Holy Spirit can now do nothing greater or more *glorious* for us than to lead us into the fellowship and likeness of that crucified life of our Lord and Savior.

Is this the reason that our prayers for the mighty working of the Holy Spirit are not more abundantly answered? Have we prayed too little that the Holy Spirit might glorify *Christ* in us in the fellowship and the conformity to His sufferings. The Spirit, who led *Christ* to the cross, is longing and is able to maintain in us the life of abiding in the crucified Jesus.

The Spirit and the cross are inseparable. The Spirit led *Christ* to the cross; the cross brought *Christ* to the throne to receive the fullness of the Spirit to impart to His people. The Spirit taught Peter to preach *Christ* crucified; it was through that preaching that three thousand received the Spirit. In the preaching of the gospel, in the Christian life, as in *Christ,* so in us, the Spirit and the cross are inseparable.

One of the great causes of the weakness of the church is the lack of the mind and disposition of the crucified *Christ* in sacrificing self and the word to win life for the dying.

May God teach us to say: We have been crucified with *Christ*; in Him we have died to sin; "Always carrying about in the body the dying of Jesus." So we will be prepared for that fullness of the Spirit which the Father longs to give.

FLESH REVEALED

"Therefore, brethren, having boldness to enter the Holiest by the blood of Jesus, by a new and living way which He consecrated for us, through the veil, that is, His flesh." (Hebrews 10:19,20)

In the temple there was a veil between the Holy Place and the Most Holy. At the altar in the court the blood of the sacrifice was sprinkled for forgiveness of sins. That gave the priest entrance into the Holy Place to offer God the incense as part of a holy worship. Behind the veil, [into the Most Holy], alone the high priest might enter once a year. That veil was the type of sinful human nature; even though it had received the forgiveness of sin, full access and fellowship with God was impossible.

When *Christ* died, the veil was rent. *Christ* dedicated a new and living way to God through the rent veil of His flesh. This new way, by which we now can enter into the Holiest of all, passes through the rent veil of the flesh. Every believer "has crucified the flesh with its passions and desires" (Galatians 5:24). Every step on the new and living way for entering into God's holy presence maintains the fellowship with the cross of *Christ*. The rent veil [let us *draw* near with a true heart in full assurance of faith, having our hearts sprinkled from an evil conscience and our bodies washed with pure water] (Hebrews 10:22) of the flesh has reference, not only to *Christ* and His sufferings, but to our experience in the *likeness* of His sufferings.

Could this be the reason why many Christians can never attain close fellowship with God? They have never yielded the flesh as an accursed thing to the condemnation of the cross. They desire to enter into the Holiest of All, and yet allow the flesh with its desires and pleasures to rule over them. God grant that we may rightly understand, in the power of the Holy Spirit, that *Christ* has called us to hate our life, to lose our life, to be dead with Him to sin that we may live to God with Him.

There is no way to a full abiding fellowship with God but through the rent veil of the flesh, through a life with the flesh crucified in *Christ Jesus*. Let us be thankful to God that the Holy Spirit dwells in us to keep the flesh in its place of crucifixion and condemnation, and to give us *victory* over all temptations.

RUN TO JESUS

"Therefore we also, since we are surrounded by so great a cloud of witnesses, let us lay aside every weight, and the sin which so easily ensnares us, and let us run with endurance the race that is set before us, looking unto Jesus, the author and finisher of our faith, who for the joy that was set before Him endured the cross, despising the shame, and has sat down at the right hand of the throne of God." (Hebrews 12:1,2)

In running a race the eye and heart are set upon the goal and the prize. The Christian is called to keep his eye fixed on Jesus enduring the cross, as the one object of imitation and desire. In our whole life we are forever to be animated by His Spirit as He bore the cross. This was the way that led to the throne and the glory of God. This is the new and living way which He opened for us through the veil of the flesh.

We realize that it was for 'His bearing the cross' that God so highly exalted Him, that we will walk in His footsteps bearing *our cross* after Him with the flesh condemned and crucified. (Please read again). The lack of spiritual feeling among some Christians is greatly owed to the fact that this cross-bearing mind of Jesus is so little preached and practiced. Most Christians think that as long as they do not commit actual sin they are at liberty to possess and enjoy as much of the world as they please. There is little insight into the deep *truth* that the world, and the flesh that loves the world, is hostel against God. It is sad that many Christians seek and pray for years for conformity to the image of Jesus, and yet fail entirely. They do not know, they do not seek with the whole heart to know, what it is to die to self and the world.

It was for the joy set before Him that *Christ* endured the cross - the joy of pleasing and glorifying the Father, the joy of loving and winning souls for Himself. We have a need of a new crusade with the proclamation: This is the will of God, that as *Christ* found His highest happiness through His endurance of the cross, and received from the Father the fullness of the Spirit to pour down on His people, so it is only in our fellowship of the cross that we can really become conformed to the image of God's Son. As believers are awaken to this truth, and run the race forever looking to the crucified Jesus, they will receive power to win for *Christ* the souls He has purchased on the cross.

Yes, the Christian race requires great commitment and focus, but has one great 'reward' that the Olympic games do not have. In the Christian race, every runner can win. Paul wrote, "Do you not know that those who run in a race all run, but one receives the prize? Run in such a way that you may obtain it.

But those who wait on the Lord Shall renew their strength; They shall mount up with wings like eagles, They shall run and not be weary, They shall walk and not faint (Isaiah 40:31). Jesus had His eye on the goal – He could see you saved. He paid the price, so that you could be saved.

Do you want to know how to run the race? Jesus is your example. Keep your eyes on Him. He is the Savior who not only shows you how to run the race, but He enters into you through the Holy Spirit, and runs the race *through* you. Praise God – we are never alone.

Listen closely as He says, "Follow Me"...

BEAR THE CROSS

"For the bodies of those animals, whose blood is brought into the sanctuary by the high priest for sin, are burned outside the camp. Therefore Jesus also, that He might sanctify the people with His own blood, suffered outside the gate. Therefore let us go forth to Him, outside the camp, bearing His reproach." (Hebrews 13:11-13)

The blood of the sin offering was brought into the Holy Place; the body of the sacrifice was burned outside the camp. Even so with *Christ.* His blood was presented to the Father; but His body was cast out as an accursed thing, outside the camp.

We read in Hebrews 10: "Let us enter into the Holy Place by the blood of Jesus." And: "Therefore let us go forth to Him, outside the camp, bearing His reproach." The deeper my insight is into the *boldness* which His blood gives me in God's presence, so much greater will be the joy with which I enter the Holy Place. And the deeper my insight is into the shame of the cross which He on my behalf bore outside the camp, the more willing I must be, in the fellowship of His cross, to follow Him outside the camp, bearing His reproach.

There are many Christians who love to hear of the boldness with which we can enter into the Holy Place through His blood who yet have little desire for the fellowship of His reproach, and are unwilling to separate themselves from the world with the same boldness with which they think to enter the Sanctuary.

The Christian suffers inconceivable loss when he thinks of entering into the Holy Place in faith and prayer, and then feels himself free to enjoy the friendship of the world, as long as he does nothing actually sinful. But the Word of God has said: "Do you not know that friendship with the world is enmity with God? (James 4:4). Whoever therefore wants to be a friend of the world makes himself an enemy of God?" "Do not love the world or the things in the world. If anyone loves the world, the love of the Father is not in him" (1 John 2:15). And do not be conformed to this world. (Romans 12:2)

To be a follower of *Christ* implies a heart given up to testify for *Christ* in the midst of the world, if by any means some may be won. To be a follower of *Christ* means to be like Him in His love of the cross and His willingness to sacrifice self that the Father may be glorified, and that men may be saved.

So to take up the cross of the reproach of *Christ* daily means that, no matter what people think of us, we must make it our day-to-day habit of conforming our choices to *Christ's* will as we know it from His word. Self denial, herein, should be the constant of our lives.

LIVE FOR RIGHTEOUSNESS

"Who Himself bore our sins in His own body on the tree, that we, having died to sins, might live for righteousness —by whose stripes you were healed." (1 Peter 2:24)

In this letter of Peter we have the same lessons that Paul has taught us. First, the atonement of the cross; "Who Himself bore our sins in His own body on the tree." And then the fellowship of the cross; "that we, having died to sins, might live for righteousness."

In this last expression we have the thought that a Christian cannot live unto righteousness except as he knows that he has died unto sin. We need the Holy Spirit to make our death to sin in *Christ* such a reality that we know ourselves to be forever free from its power, and so surrender our members to God as instruments of righteousness. These words give us a short summary of the teaching of Romans 6. Don't you know that when you offer yourselves to someone to obey him as slaves, you are slaves to the one whom you obey-whether you are slaves to sin, which leads to death, or to obedience, leading to righteousness?

It cost *Christ* much to bear the cross, and then to surrender Himself for it to bear Him. It cost Him much when He cried: "Now My soul is troubled, and what shall I say? 'Father, save Me from this hour'? But for this *purpose* I came to this hour." (John 12:27)

Peter speaks here in the fellowship of the cross, [of which], "we, having died to sins, might live for righteousness," is easily understood or experienced. It means that the Holy Spirit will teach us what it is to be identified with *Christ* in His cross. It means that we realize by faith how actually we shared with *Christ* in His death, and now, as He *lives* in us, abiding in fellowship with Him, the Crucified One. This costs self- sacrifice; it costs earnest prayer; it costs a whole-hearted surrender to God and His will and the cross of Jesus; it costs abiding in *Christ*, and fellowship with Him.

Let us know today [now] that *Christ* is in us and we are in *Christ*. *Christ* now lives in us the life that was crucified and now is glorified in heaven. Let your Spirit burn the words deep into our hearts. Having died unto sin, and being forever set free from its dominion, let us know that sin can no more reign over us, or have dominion. Let us in the power of your redemption yield ourselves unto God as those who are alive from the dead, ready and prepared for all His will.

FOLLOWERS OF CHRIST

"By this we know love, because He laid down His life for us. And we also ought to lay down our lives for the brethren." (1 John 3:16)

"Greater love hath no man than this, that a man lay down his life [soul] for his friends." (John 15:13). Our Lord reveals to us the love that moved Him to die for us. And now under the influence and in the power of this love dwelling in us, comes the message: "And we also ought to lay down our lives for the brethren." Therefore nothing is expected of us than a *Christ*-like life and a *Christ*-like love, proving itself in all our dealings with our brethren.

The cross of *Christ* is the measure by which we know how much *Christ* loves us. That cross is the measure of the love we owe to the brethren around us. It is only as the love of *Christ* on the cross possesses our hearts, and *daily* renews our whole being, that we should be able to love our brethren. Our fellowship in the cross of *Christ* is to manifest itself in our sacrifice of love, not only to *Christ* Himself, but to all who belong to Him.

The life in which John speaks to us is something entirely supernatural and divine. It is only the faith of *Christ* Himself living in us that can enable us to accept this great command in the assurance that *Christ* Himself will work it *out* in us.

It is He who calls us: "If anyone desires to come after Me, let him deny himself, and take up his cross, and follow Me" (Matthew 16:24). Nothing less than this, a dying to our own nature, a faith that our "old man," our flesh has been crucified with *Christ*, so that we no longer need to sin - nothing less than this can enable us to say: "For this is the love of God, that we keep His commandments. And His commandments are not burdensome [difficult] ." (1 John 5:3)

But for such fellowship and conformity to the death of *Christ*, nothing will avail but the daily, unbroken abiding in *Christ* Jesus which He has promised us. By the Holy Spirit revealing and glorifying *Christ* in us, we may trust *Christ* to live out His life in us.

He proved His love on the cross of Calvary, He Himself, He alone can enable us to say in truth: By this we know love, because He laid down His life for us. And we also should lay down our lives for the brethren.

Because all that is in the world, lust of the flesh, desire of the body, vain glory of life: empty pride, boast, and display of material things of the present life is not of the Father but is of the world

I pray the indwelling *Christ* obtains His place in the faith of the Church, that the *Christ*-like love to the brethren will become the mark of true Christianity, by which all men will know that we are of *Christ*. This will bring help to the world in believing that God has loved us even as He loved *Christ*.

THE LAMB LEADS

"These are the ones who follow the Lamb wherever He goes." (Revelation 14:4)

We are sure, that it will be the counterpart in glory of what it is to follow in the footsteps of the Lamb here upon earth. As the Lamb on earth reveals what the Lamb in heaven would be, so His followers on earth can show forth something of the glory [of 'one similar to a son of man'] of what it is to follow Him in heaven.

How may the footsteps of the Lamb be known? "He humbled Himself." "Yet He opened not His mouth; He was led as a lamb to the slaughter," (Isaiah 53:7). It is the meekness and gentleness and humility that marked Him which calls for His followers to *walk* in His footsteps.

Our Lord Himself said: " Take My yoke upon you and learn from Me, for I am gentle and lowly in heart, and you will find rest for your souls" (Matthew 11:29). Paul writes: "Let this mind be in you which was also in Christ Jesus" (Philippians 2:5). And then he teaches us: Being in the form of God, He emptied Himself; He was made in the likeness of men; He took the form of a servant; He humbled Himself; He became obedient unto death, even the death of the cross.

The Lamb is our Lord and Lawgiver. He opened the only path that leads to the throne of God. As we learn from Him what it means to be meek and lowly, what it means to empty ourselves, to choose the place of the servant, to humble ourselves and become obedient, even unto death, the death of the cross, that we shall *find* the new and living way that leads us into the Holiest of All.

"Therefore God also has highly exalted Him and given Him the name which is above every name" (Phil 2:9). The Lord humbled Himself to the uttermost, but God exalted Him to the highest peak.

Let Paul's words be the keynote of your life: "I have been crucified with *Christ*; it is no longer I who live, but *Christ* lives in me" You have the way to follow the *Christ* to the glory of God in heaven.

Please note that there has not been a name [any other name] on this earth above the name of Jesus!

GLORY TO HIM

"And from Jesus *Christ,* the faithful witness, the firstborn from the dead, and the ruler over the kings of the earth. To Him who loved us and washed [freed] us from our sins in His own blood, and has made us kings [kingdom] and priests to His God and Father, to Him be glory and dominion forever and ever. Amen." (Revelation 1:5,6)

Some may feel that it is not easy to understand the meaning of the cross, or to carry it out in their lives. Do not think of it as a heavy burden or yoke that you have to bear? *Christ* says: "My yoke is easy, and My burden is light." His love makes everything easy. Don't think of your love to Him, but of His great love for you. You have assurance that Jesus *Christ* loves you. It is through the love of *Christ* on the cross that souls are *drawn* to Him.

We have the answer to what will enable us to love the fellowship of the crucified Jesus. His love is poured out through the continual breathing of the Holy Spirit into the heart of every child of God. "To Him who loves us" - that our souls may enter in, and find there their everlasting dwelling-place. This everlasting love seeks to take possession of you and fill you with joy.

"And has released us from our sins in His blood" - this is proof enough that He will never *reject* me; that I am *precious* in His sight, and through the power of His blood I am *well-pleasing* to God?

"And made us a kingdom, priests to His God and Father" - and now preserves us by His power, and will strengthen us through His Spirit to reign as kings over sin and the world, and to appear as priests before God in intercession for others. As we turn to Him and surrender day by day, let us say: "To Him be glory and dominion forever and ever. Amen."

We the followers of *Christ* have not only been redeemed by the blood of *Christ,* born of God into His kingdom, but have been made a kingdom [church]. All reborn believers are a part of this kingdom. God is recovering His right over the earth in order to make it His kingdom. When *Christ* came He brought the kingdom of God with Him. This kingdom has been enlarged in the church which will establish the kingdom of God on the whole earth and coming through the overcoming of believers.

Redemption through *Christ's* blood made us a kingdom and priest to God. The kingdom is God's dominion and the priests are the expression of God's image.

CROSS BLESSES YOU

But God forbid that I should boast except in the cross of our Lord Jesus *Christ*, by whom [the cross] the world has been crucified to me, and I to the world." (Galatians 6:14)

One of the blessings of the cross consists in this, that it teaches us to know the worthlessness of our efforts and the corruption of our own nature. The cross does not offer to improve human nature, or to supply what man is unable to do.

Many people, indeed, use it in this way, by putting a patch over the old self to improve the self image. This develops confusion as they are constantly walking from minister to another without finding what they seek. No, the old self, our old man, must be laid aside, and given over to the death of the cross. And the cross causes all that of the 'lost nature of man' to die the accursed death, and the 'I' takes the place of a malefactor; it breaks the staff over all that is of the old nature.

Whosoever has been brought to the cross through the Spirit has learned to pronounce the death sentence on his old nature and has broken the staff over himself. He that would save his life remains under the curse. If we have learned through the Spirit to understand the cross, then we have lost our life and will no longer expect any good from our old nature, and will not judge others, but only ourselves.

But as long as we have not been taught this lesson [through the Spirit], we will try to find good in ourselves, something of worth in God's sight, and which the sentence of death will not be passed. And if we find nothing at all, we fall into a false grief which the Evil One [Satan] eagerly uses to make us despair, by saying: "You might as well give up. God will not trouble with you. There is nothing for you but failure."

This is not what God desires. What we possess by nature must be nailed to the cross and we *must* put on the new man. The cross brings man to utter failure [bankruptcy] of himself, and then God can come to our aid. The cross brought the disciples of Jesus once to such an end of themselves, which even the words of the Master had failed to do. It took from them the aureole [circle of light]of holiness which they thought they had won in the three years they followed Jesus, and it taught them to know themselves.

And so they were prepared to receive the Holy Spirit, who would impart a new nature and a new life. For we cannot separate the cross from the Spirit. We have no Easter and no Pentecost until we first have a Good Friday.

Through the cross alone are we prepared for life in the fullness of God; only he who is crucified with *Christ* can be a vessel unto honor.

Our 'old man' must be crucified with *Christ* (Romans 6:6), and in the resurrection of *Christ* we find the roots of our new life (1 Peter 1:3). Whosoever loses his life shall find it. We must learn the lesson of the cross as condemned and rejected ones, who have been crucified with *Christ*. Then the door will be open for a life of power and blessing. All that belongs to death must be given over *to* death, even as the body is laid away in the earth because it *belongs* to the earth.

The world has been crucified to us and we to the world. This has taken place through *Christ* who was crucified. Paul dealt with religious people who were concerned for the things of God but were misguided by their religion that had become a world.

By the cross we are 'separated from the *religious* world' and are now qualified to live the new creation.

The Holy Spirit, the Eternal Spirit, is unchangeable. He brought *Christ* our Head to the cross, and us [His children] with Him. For this work in us is twofold. On the one hand it leads us to death, and all that belongs to death; and on the other hand, to that life which God has placed within us, and which leads from glory to glory.

Praise God for the gift of the Holy Spirit, who will reveal to me the secret of the cross of *Christ*! The Spirit strengthened *Christ* to offer Himself to God on the cross. The cross gave *Christ* the right to receive the fullness of the Spirit from the Father to pour out on *all* flesh. The cross gives us the right to receive the Spirit. And the Spirit teaches us to love the cross, and to partake of the life crucified with *Christ.*

CHOICE OF THE CROSS

As you at the cross what do you see? Do you see a choice? We all have a choice to make. Have you ever thought about your eternal choice?

As we look at the three crosses we see the giver of life in between two criminals that have a choice. Isn't it great to have someone that loves us so much that we are not forced, but we are allowed to make the *choice.*

There are those that mock at God, just as one did on the cross, and there are those that accept the free gift of God's love through His Son, Jesus. The free gift of eternal life. Wow! What a choice. And praise to the other one that saw the *same* Jesus on the cross and he prayed for Him. Jesus loved them both and gave both the same choice.

It saddens me that some can accept eternal life and some reject it. He allows you the same choice.

THE LORD'S PRAYER

Our Father in heaven,

Hallowed be Your name.

Your kingdom come.

Your *will* be done

On earth as it is in heaven.

Give us this day our daily bread.

And forgive us our debts,

As we forgive our debtors.

And do not lead us into temptation,

But deliver us from the evil one.

For Yours is the kingdom and the power and the glory
forever. Amen

Ask our Heavenly Father to increase His Kingdom in you
so with His guidance you can help to spread the Kingdom
of God on earth.

Mackey

Ask.   Seek.   Knock.

GATE WILL OPEN

Have you passed through that narrow gate? Trusted in the Lord Jesus *Christ* as the door of salvation? Do you believe in Him as the way, the truth, and the life? (John 14:6) Is the Word of God your foundation and your guide?

Jesus made it clear that there are only two gates, only two paths, only two destinies before every man, and each of us must choose one or the other. Jesus narrows our choices to only two: religion and *Christianity*. Religion is defined as man's efforts to reach God, while *Christianity* is God reaching down to man. Religion rests upon man's work for God; *Christianity* on God's work on behalf of men.

CHRISTIANITY

Christianity is a religion based upon the *teachings* of Jesus of Nazareth, who lived in Palestine during the first century. However, if Christianity is lived as merely a set of teachings and rules to be followed, it misses the main points that Jesus taught. First and foremost, Christianity is *anchored* in love-God's love for us and our response to that love. We will examine what is Christianity and how it should be lived by those who profess to be its followers.

Many skeptics think that religion is a waste of time. I tend to agree. I am a Christian, but I don't consider myself a particularly religious person. Christianity is much *more* than just religion.

BASIS OF CHRISTIANITY

Christianity was derived from Judaism. Under Judaism, the Hebrew Old Testament writings formed the basis of a covenant between God (Yahweh) and the people of Israel. According to the prophecies found in those writings, God was going to send the Messiah (anointed One), who would bless not only the Israelites, but *all humanity* of the world. Jesus' purpose was two-fold:

First, according to both Old and New Testament writings, Jesus was God, who took on human form to teach us about Himself and His path to salvation (eternal life).

Second, Jesus was to provide the ultimate sacrifice (death on a Roman cross) for sins (the bad things we do), so that we could be with Him forever in heaven. To prove that He was God and that the sacrifice was effective, Jesus *rose* from the dead.

So, according to Christianity, Jesus is the *Christ,* the Messiah-the fulfillment of the Old Testament prophecies and God of all.

TEACHINGS OF JESUS

Jesus did not teach anything radically different from that of the Old Testament, He simplified the main points so that people could *not* escape into a pure exercise of religious ceremonies.

The Old Testament describes many laws (both moral and ceremonial) that were to be followed by the people of God. With so many laws, people tended to become selective, preferring to follow the easier ceremonial laws over the more difficult moral laws. (Matthew 23:23)

The religious ruling class was especially sensitive to selective obedience of the law, resulting in moral hypocrisy. Jesus explained that the moral commandments were not to be followed merely to the letter of the law, but also to the intent of the law. So, it was not enough to abstain from adultery, but God required that one not even look on a woman with lust. (Matthew 5:27-28)

It is not enough to abstain from murder, but God requires that nobody hate another without cause, with calling another person 'a fool' making one guilty enough to suffer the judgment of Hell (Matthew 5:21-22). So God's laws require not only perfect performance, but also perfect attitude and motive.

Jesus said the entire law of God could be summarized into a mere two commands:

Jesus replied: "'Love the Lord your God with *all* your heart and with *all* your soul and with *all* your mind.' This is the first and greatest commandment.

And the second is like it: 'Love your neighbor as yourself.' All the Law and the Prophets hang on these two commandments." (Matthew 22:37-40)

So, the fundamental principle that defines the Christian experience is love-love of God and love of our fellow human beings. So, a person who merely loves his fellow man is only fulfilling half of the law, and is neglecting what Jesus said was the most important part-*loving* God.

*The image of God is **love**.*

SALVATION

Since God's standard for behavior is perfection in thought and deed, we are going to find it very difficult to meet God's standard. However, since God loves us so much, He has provided another means by which we can attain perfection.

Jesus, as God, took on the form of a human being and lived on the earth in the first century. Besides teaching, His main purpose was to provide the ultimate sacrifice for sins, by living a completely sinless life, dying on a cross, and rising from the dead. It is through belief in Jesus and His sacrifice for sins that one is declared *righteous and free* from sin. One who believes in Jesus follows Him, being indwelt by the Holy Spirit, who guides Christians as they become *conformed to the image* of *Christ.*

Before we can examine whether a believer can be secure in his salvation, we need to understand how we are saved according to the Bible, God's Word. In many religions it is believed that a person goes to heaven if one's good deeds outweigh ones bad deeds. The Bible says that sins (bad deeds) keep a person out of heaven, regardless of good deeds, since God is completely without sin and *cannot* have fellowship with a sinner.

When Jesus first taught this concept, the disciples were astonished and asked "Who then can be saved?" Jesus' response was "With man this is impossible, but with God *all* things are possible." (Matthew 19:26)

The Bible says that salvation is a work of God, based upon belief in Jesus *Christ.* Although the concept of belief seems simple and straightforward, it involves more than just an acknowledgment that Jesus existed in history, since even the demons believe.

You believe that there is one God? Did you know that even the demons believe that? (James 2:19)

The difference between a true believer and a demon is that although the demon mentally understands the concept, he *rejects* the 'lordship' of Jesus *Christ.* Likewise, a 'Christian' who responded to an altar call in 1966, but isn't *following* Jesus isn't really a believer. The New Testament qualifies the definition of a believer as being one who has faith in Jesus *Christ.* Faith is more than merely having some knowledge about the facts surrounding the life and teaching of Jesus *Christ.* Jesus Himself said that those who truly believed in Him would 'take up his cross' and follow Him.

The Bible calls into question the 'belief' of anyone who is not following Jesus as Lord. Another sign of a true believer is that the believer does not *practice* sin (live in a state of continual sin) (1 John 3:9-10), although we are not completely without sin. (Romans 3:23)

Many critics of 'once saved always saved' object to what they call easy belief-ism. Much of the emphasis in Christian evangelism is on the 'altar call' or 'revival meeting.' Although some people can be saved, (such as I) many are caught up in the *emotion* of the moment and do not really *believe*. Then they wonder why their lives have not changed. It is clear from the Bible that the true believer is transformed through the *power* of the Holy Spirit.

SANCTIFICATION

We look in the dictionary and find the meaning of sanctification: "is an ancient concept widespread among religions that refers to anything blessed or set apart for special purposes, from totem poles to temple vessels, to the change brought about in a human." Most believe it is the process by which a Christian becomes more and more like Jesus. Perfection is not possible in this world, but God wants us to love Him and our fellow human beings more. (Matthew 22:37-40)

So, a Christian's life is not over once you make a commitment to Jesus. To be a fulfilled Christian, a follower of Jesus is to study the Bible, the source of God's word to His people. In addition, Christians are to attend a fellowship of other believers on a regular basis for instruction, fellowship, worship, and service. This helps in growing in faith, knowledge of God's Word, and to *follow* Him.

God has prepared ahead of time a lifetime of good works that we should do (Ephesians 2:10), which fulfills both great commandments-love of God and love of our fellow human beings.

In Revelation 22:12, Jesus says, "My reward is with me, and I will give to everyone according to what he has done." Of course, the verse is about rewards given to believers, which is independent of obtaining salvation. Believers receive rewards in heaven based upon good deeds ('what he has done') performed on earth, although these deeds [rewards] do *not* get one into heaven.

UNIQUE RELIGION

Christianity is *more* than a religion. Christianity is a way of life based upon one's love of God and love of people. Christianity is also a commitment to personal integrity and truth. It's a way of doing the *works* of Jesus.

So God is perfect and we are imperfect (*all* humanity). Mankind can only create imperfect religions. This means that all man-created religions hold common characteristics. This means that the one religion created by God is unique, because it has *only* the characteristics that God could give it.

Christianity, because it was created by God, is a unique religion.

Here are some examples:

In Christianity salvation is a free gift given to us by God. In all other religions you achieve salvation through good works or good thoughts.

In no other religion does the leader die so that his followers may be saved, and then return after death to demonstrate the eternal life we can have.

Christianity is the only religion in which love, including love for your enemies, is the central theme.

Christianity offers assurance of heaven and eternal life.

Christianity is the only religion in which God personally suffers with mankind.

ENTER THE GATE

What is a gate? We go through a gate to get to what is on the other side. What does a gate do? A gate gives us *access* to something. Jesus is saying that it is through Him we get to heaven. Of course, through Him we are saved. I am the door. [gate] If anyone enters by Me, he will be saved, and will go in and out and find pasture. (John 10:9)

Christ is the the doorway not only through which God' elect may go in but also through which His chosen people may go out. In John 10:7 Jesus said to them again, "Most assuredly, I say to you, I am the door of the sheep."

The pasture here (10:9) signifies *Christ* as the feeding place for the sheep. When the pasture is not available the sheep are kept in the fold. When the pasture is ready, there is no need for the sheep to remain in the fold. To be kept in the fold is transitional and temporary. To be in the pasture enjoying its riches is final and permanent.

Before *Christ* came, the law was a ward, and being under the law was transitional. Now that *Christ* has come, all God's chosen people must come out of the law and come into Him to enjoy Him as their pasture. (Galatians 3:23-25; 4:3-5)

What is a fold? At night sheep are brought to a holding area known as a fold. Several shepherds may use the same fold. So there may be three or four herds in the same fold. The sheep will be kept and guarded in the fold.

The next morning each shepherd will come to the gate of the fold. He will step outside of the gate and *call* his sheep. The sheep will have mingled during the night. Each shepherd's sheep are not all together but mixed in with all of the other herds. But when the shepherd calls, his sheep will all come forward and *follow* him. Not one of his sheep will stay in the fold. The same thing happens as each shepherd steps out and calls his sheep.

The sheep will only follow their shepherd's voice. They will not respond to another shepherd's voice. Someone can try to mimic the shepherd's voice but the sheep know the difference. Someone can dress up to look like the shepherd but the sheep know by his voice that it is not their shepherd.

In John 10:3-5 we read, "To him the doorkeeper opens, and the sheep hear his voice; and he calls his own sheep by name and leads them out. And when he brings out his own sheep, he goes before them; and the sheep follow him, for they know his voice. Yet they will by no means follow a stranger, but will flee from him, for they do not know the voice of strangers."

If we obey Jesus and follow His words, then we are His sheep. We will only follow and obey Him. If someone comes along and calls us to follow them we will not do it. We will know that they are not speaking with the voice of Jesus. We will know that they are not our Shepherd.

If you want to enter God's kingdom, do not follow the crowds, instead follow the light of the cross. I pray you remain safe in the *shadow* of the cross and may you reach the throne of God and have Him say,"Well done, good and faithful *servant* enter into the joy of your Master".

Mackey

A MYSTERY

Why are you here? What purpose is your life and what are you to do? Are you chained to this earth?

God's plan is for us to become His Son and Daughter.

To reach this we must do as Jesus did by carrying our cross. We must follow in His footsteps that are laid out in our path.

God has a reward for those that follow *Christ*...because you are of Him and lost without Him.

The moment you cried out to *Christ* He looked inside Himself and saw you. Why are you there? Because you are in Him before, at the beginning, and at the end. No matter where you are, you are always in Him.

He found you at the end, and He saw your name in the Book of Life *before* the beginning. At that 'non-time' He elected you, chose you, justified you, sanctified you and glorified you. See your [dimensionless] Lord, with creation in Him.

God looks upon *you*, His creation and smiles because you are beautiful to Him and in Him you are perfect, flawless, honored, holy, and forever pure because you are in Christ in the beginning, and in Him you made it to the end.

Jesus *Christ* is before creation and after creation. *Christ* and ALL the parts of *Christ* are the content of the new creation.

You are the content of that new creation. The best part of you is not a creation. Your body is a thing created. It ends when the old creation ends and is then completely replaced by a translated body.

Your spirit is not of this realm. Your spirit is from the other realm. One-third of you is in the invisible realm. *Christ* has placed Himself in you, in that one-third of you. Your spirit and His spirit have become one.

Christ is in you as you are in Him. A part of you is not of this creation and in this 'part' of you is life. It is referred to as Eternal Life. That life is *Christ*!

When you believed on *Christ*, two things happened to you. First, your spirit was raised from the dead. Second, *Christ* made His spirit one with your spirit. This *Christ*, who now lives beyond death cannot die.

Christ chose you before foundation of the world. *Christ* is the first. *Christ* was and is...the real lamb. All creation is but a picture *Christ*.

This glorious Lord with all creation in Him, this Lord who finished all things before He created all things, this Lord who chose you in Himself before the foundation of the world, this Lord who wrote your name in the Book of Life, this *Christ* who was slain, this *Christ* who is the glory of the Father, this *Christ* who is the ALL, who will be, and is, the ALL who is in ALL, this *Christ* who is the beginning and end, this *Christ* who is free of, above and beyond and outside of ALL space, time, and even eternity...this *Christ* Lives in You!

It was God's will to make known what are the riches of the glory of the mystery, and to make known to you that this *Christ*-the *Christ* before creation, the *Christ* beyond creation-this *Christ* dwells in you.

This awesome , endless, immense *Christ* is living in you *right now*!

Upon what is the church built? The church is built on a revelation of this Lord, this *Christ*.

The mystery which has been hidden from ages and from generations, but now has been revealed to His saints (Colossians 1:26). "Nevertheless do not rejoice in this, that the spirits are subject to you, but rather rejoice because your names are written in heaven." (Luke 2:20)

And they said, "Is not this Jesus, the son of Joseph, whose father and mother we know? How is it then that He says, 'I have come down from heaven'?" (John 6:42)

Your father Abraham rejoiced to see My day, and he saw it and was glad. (John 8:58)

While we do not look at the things which are seen, but at the things which are not seen. For the things which are seen are temporary, but the things which are not seen are eternal. (2 Corinthians 4:18)

Because of the hope which is laid up for you in heaven, of which you heard before in the word of the truth of the gospel. (Colossians 1:5)

He is the image of the invisible God, the firstborn over all creation. For by Him all things were created that are in heaven and that are on earth, visible and invisible, whether thrones or dominions or principalities or powers. All things were created through Him and for Him (Colossians 1:15-16). And He is before all things, and in Him all things consist. (Colossians 1:17)

Blessed be the God and Father of our Lord Jesus *Christ*, who has blessed us with every spiritual blessing in the heavenly places in *Christ*. (Ephesian.1:3)

For our citizenship is in heaven, from which we also eagerly wait for the Savior, the Lord Jesus *Christ*, who will transform our lowly body that it may be conformed to His glorious body, according to the working by which He is able even to subdue all things to Himself. (Philippians 3:20-21)

In hope of eternal life which God, who cannot lie, promised before time began. (Titus 1:2)

Who being the brightness of His glory and the express image of His person, and upholding all things by the word of His power, when He had by Himself purged our sins, sat down at the right hand of the Majesty on high. (Hebrews 1:3)

This is the realm of the spirituals, the natural habitat of your Lord.

Your Lord abides in a realm where all things are the eternal now. So also does your spirit.

It is in this realm that you touch the Lord. The New Testament makes reference to this realm, but it is often overlooked. This is because some of us have a very objective view of our faith.

I have often spoken of this door to this realm. As I have visioned it, seen it, and went through it. He wants you to seek Him and you will find the door, you will understand the Spirit within you, and you will learn as He shows you this path and this realm by His Word. He is always waiting to take your hand in His and walk together. As you begin to see this Christian faith from the other realm, may you begin to become aware that two realms join; and the joining of your Lord and your spirit is the doorway between those two realms.

Do you understand this mystery? God wants a relationship with you, *not* a man-made religion. Give Him your heart and He *will* change it.

Let your faith continue to grow in *Christ*. Let your soul feed daily upon the Living Word of God. The very Word that created all [is all] and in all.

Seven years ago I was personally invited to a pastors' home, and upon arriving the first set of words he spoke to me were: "Isn't it great that *Christ* is in us." Out of his excitement, I thought it was a question and then realized it was a statement to proclaim what actually resided in us. Thank you Pastor Jonathan Ray Smith for helping me to get on the path to the meaning of the 'true' lighthouse.

I did not know at that moment a *search* would take place to find and understand the true meaning: the mystery of this *Christ* in us.

This is for you, who once was like me seeking *more* of Him. All of Him.

May you continue to *seek* Him with *all* your heart.

WORLD OF IMAGE

First of all, according to the Scriptures *all* physical things, all the material things that we see, touch, and enjoy, are not the real things. They are but a shadow, a figure of the true. Day by day we are contacting so many material objects: we are eating food, drinking water, putting on clothes; we are living in our houses and driving in our cars. These things are not real.

They are but shadows, figures. The food we take every day is not the real food but a figure of the real. The water we drink is not the real water. The light before our eyes is not the real light but a figure *pointing* to something else.

We live in a world of shadows, symbols, types, images and pictures.

We speak of gold; but the gold we have here in the material realm is made of mass, filled with protons, electrons and atoms, in a place that gives us no more than a picture of real gold. Real gold is *Christ*. Our gold, here in the realm of mass, is a suggestion of *Christ.*

The *real* sun is *Christ*. Our sun is a shadow of *Christ. It* is a picture of Him.

ALL is made of *Christ*. And creation was strewn with pictures of Him. That moon up in the sky is not the true reality. That moon is a picture of *Christ.*

Then what are the *real* things? Before creation there existed in the Father, in the Son, and in the Holy Spirit the *real* gold, the real water, and real food.

There in God resided *real* water, food, light and life; and they are not shadows, nor symbols, nor images, nor reflections.

So the real things are nothing but *Christ* Himself. *Christ* is the real food to us. *Christ* is the real water to us. *Christ* is the real light to us. *Christ* is the reality of everything to us. Even our physical life is not a real life. It is but a figure pointing to *Christ*. *Christ* is the real life to us. If you don't have *Christ,* you don't have life. You will say, "I am living; I have life in my body!" But you must realize that this is not the real life. It is merely a shadow *pointing* to the real life which is *Christ* Himself.

Life was *Christ.* True Life is *Christ!* All we have here in this physical creation is a *shadow* of Life. *Christ* is Life!

Before creation began, *Christ* was everything, and everything was *Christ.*

You and I and ALL things around us are shadows, pictures, images, replicas, and reflections of *Christ*.

Praise God for the true follower's of *Christ.* Praise Him for us that are able to step out of the present realm into the spiritual realm and dwell together with *Christ*. To be lead by *Christ* and in communion with one another.

So many dwell on the paradise to come, only to miss out at the golden truth of the beauty which dwells within themselves. That beauty is *Christ* Himself!

That *Christ* is in them, in you, in me, in everything right now! You need to know that *everything* you need is *inside* you. You are in the eternals of the flowing river of the true life.

Paul gives us the key to this mystery in 1 Corinthians 6:17: "He that is joined to the Lord is one spirit." When the spirit leaves the body, the body disintegrates. It loses its structure because it is always dependent upon the spirit for its organization of reality. The spirit has independent reality. The body has only relative reality. It is the spirit that gives life and sustains the body.

So, the spirit is essential reality and the material is only accidental, or has only relative reality. In other words, your spirit is the real 'you', the real person. A person who is *joined to the Lord as one spirit* is, in his essential being, seated with *Christ* in the heavens.

While the body is here, the real self is there. A body may occupy only one place at a time, the spirit is not so confined. Because "he that is joined to the Lord is one spirit," therefore, since *Christ* is exalted and enthroned, the Church is exalted and enthroned with Him.

To reach this you *must* step out on faith to increase the spiritual awareness of this *Christ* in you.

CHRIST LIFE

We see that *Christ* is the Redeemer and the Savior. For *Christ* to be our Savior, He must be our life and resurrection. We now come to life [Life Giving Spirit], *Christ* being life and resurrection. As we hear the truth, we should also see the light [revelation].

Christ is not only our Redeemer but also our Savior. If we know these two aspects of what *Christ* is, when we speak of *Christ* being our Savior or our saving Lord, we will not have a superficial and narrow understanding. His saving includes redemption and salvation. Redemption is an outward saving through the efficacy of the Lord's precious blood; salvation is an inward saving by the operation of the Lord as the Spirit of life.

According to God's righteous law, a fallen man is a condemned criminal who is doomed to death and perdition. He is destined to go first to Hades and then to the lake of fire for eternal punishment. Such a criminal needs a Substitute who can pay the ransom for him and satisfy God's righteous requirement.

The Lord Jesus was God who became flesh, putting on a body of flesh and blood to become a man. He died for us with a genuine body, and He shed real human blood for us on the cross. The blood He shed was genuine human blood which can redeem sinners. This blood fully *paid* the ransom for us. Therefore, according to the procedure of His righteous law, God could proclaim forgiveness. In this way we were redeemed, and God forgave us. This is an outward matter.

The outward redemption first includes: redemption for sins; second: forgiveness of sins; third: washing of sins; fourth: justification; and fifth: reconciliation.

This is God's complete redemption. *Christ* died and shed His blood to *fully* pay the ransom for us and make redemption for our sins. Based on *Christ's* redemption, God could declare that there is forgiveness of sin; therefore, our sins were forgiven.

Then following the forgiveness of sins is the washing of sins. Forgiveness is to do away with the punishment for sins, whereas washing is to wipe out the traces of sins. We have received redemption for our sins and our sins have been washed away; therefore, we have no problem before God.

God has justified us and we have been reconciled to God with a complete change toward Him. This is God's full redemptive work.

However, as *fallen* human beings, we not only have an outward position that is condemned before God, but we also have a sinful nature *within.*

The salvation of the Lord Jesus is complete; it deals not only with our outward problem but also with our inward problem. This is because a fallen man is not only a criminal with a record of sins before God but also a sinner with the sinful nature within him. Since the nature of Satan has entered into us, we need to be saved from our sinful nature. However, God carries out His salvation not outwardly by exercising His mighty arm but inwardly by coming *into* us.

The inward salvation first includes: regeneration; second: sanctification; third: transformation: fourth: conformation; and fifth: glorification.

The outward redemption is by the effectiveness of the blood, whereas the inward salvation is through the operation of the Spirit.

Once we believe in the Lord, we receive outward redemption. As long as we believe with our *heart* and confess with our *mouth* the name of the Lord, we receive redemption for sins, forgiveness of sins, washing of sins, justification, and reconciliation.

Immediately we obtain God's complete redemption, which is outward. However, to obtain God's full salvation inwardly is both a daily devotion in following the crucified Christ. From the time of our regeneration when *Christ* came into us to be our life, He has been sanctifying us within every day. Just as tea leaves 'tea-ify' water into tea-water, so *Christ* is 'Christ-ifying' us every day to make us *Christ*-men. This is the work of sanctification. When *Christ* sanctifies us within continually, we are being *transformed* and at the same time we are being *conformed* to His likeness.

Eventually, we will be glorified. This is the procedure of the growth in life. Today *Christ* is sanctifying, transforming, and conforming us continually until we see Him in our glorification.

THE LIVING WATER

As a younger man I recall singing a song, 'deep and wide, there's a fountain growing deep and wide.' The Lord said that the water He gives will be [in us] a *well* of water, a fountain, springing up unto the life of eternity. He told us that out of the innermost part of those who believe on Him will *flow* rivers of living water.

When you are dry and thirsty in the inner man, you come to the Lord, you contact Him and you are refreshed. The supply of the *life* of *Christ* is just as living water within you.

Do you know that there is a spring within me, and not only a spring, but a *fountain* of deep water? I am full of water, so *something* is flowing forth. We have a spring, a fountain, and a stream. The spring is the source, the fountain is the storage, and the stream is the *flowing* forth.

There is a stream of wisdom, a stream of understanding, a stream of light, a stream of love, a stream of comfort, a stream of peace, a stream of joy, a stream of prayer, a stream of praise. There are many kinds of heavenly supplies.

With the living *Christ* we can love others just as a living stream flowing forth. Our patience is flowing as a stream all the time, and we *water* others.

Have you ever wondered how someone can continually speak and write without material? There is a stream in us which is *connected* with the spring in the heavens. You can never exhaust this spring. The more the living water flows out, the more the fresh supply flows in. The more I speak, the more I have to speak. If I stop speaking, it stops coming. This stream is flowing *all* the time.

When you are thirsty, it means that your spirit, your inner man is dry. But when you contact the 'living well' of *Christ* Jesus, you feel watered and your thirst is quenched. You are refreshed more by this drink than by any physical beverage. Then by contacting the Lord more and more, [moment by moment], you will feel more than watered; there will be a stream *flowing* forth from within you.

Day by day we *need* water, so something is flowing forth.

There is a stream, a stream of *ministry.*

GOD'S OFFER

God created Adam without sin. Adam; however, voluntarily rebelled against God. This rebellion is called sin. As a sinner, all of Adam's offspring are born with a sin nature. We are also sinners by our practice. We sin against God in many ways: in thoughts, in words, and in actions. Sin is vile and wicked in the sight of our Holy

God. God is so perfectly Righteous that He will *not* have fellowship with unrighteousness. God is so Just that He must punish sin.

We have made ourselves the enemies of God. Our sin has separated us from Him. There is *nothing* we can do to reconcile ourselves to God. God alone can reconcile us to Himself. Because of His Love and His Goodness, God has done the only thing that could be done to reconcile us to Him. God, the Eternal Son, became flesh in the Person of the Lord Jesus *Christ.* He lived a perfect life and then offered Himself up as a sacrifice to receive the punishment we deserve for our sin.

Jesus, who was sinless, took the full penalty for our sin through His suffering and death on the cross.

God's *justice* was satisfied and the Lord Jesus *Christ* rose from the dead. The Lord Jesus *Christ* has purchased and provided our reconciliation to God.

God has declared that all who will abandon their way and trust solely in the Lord Jesus *Christ* will be forgiven of every sin, will be credited with *Christ*'s righteousness, and will therefore be reconciled to God.

Jesus says, "For whosoever will save his life shall *lose* it." If you continue in your self-absorbed and self-willed way, the end result will be that you will *lose* your life eternally.

But, Jesus says, "whosoever will *lose* his life for My sake shall find it." If you are willing to lay down your life and follow Jesus, you will *find* eternal life.

Will you have Jesus? Will you have Him alone? Or, will you hold onto your way? In your strength? You can not have both your way and Jesus' way. If your soul is to be saved, you must *deny* yourself, take up your cross, and follow Him. Jesus alone. That is the *only* way you can come to Jesus. And it is only through Jesus that your soul can be saved.

You have a *choice,* Heaven or Hell, and you *will* meet Jesus one way or another. I pray it's the highway to heaven for you.

ENJOY GOD

We must till our spiritual ground; we must sow the spiritual seed; we must water the spiritual plants—all the time. We cannot rely upon others to do it for us; we must do it ourselves, or it will never be done.

Whenever we come to worship the Lord, we should not come with our hands empty. We must come with our hands full of the produce of *Christ*. We have to labor upon *Christ* day by day so that we produce Him in mass production. We need more than just a little of *Christ* to satisfy our own needs. We must produce enough of Him so that there will be a surplus for others, for the poor and for the needy: "You must open your hand to your brother, to the poor one with you and to the needy one with you in your land." (Deut. 15:11)

If you will live in the Lord, laboring upon Him, applying Him, and enjoying Him. If you do this, consider how fruitful and how beautiful your 'farm' will be. The farm of *Christ* in your daily life will be full of produce. When the Lord's Day comes and you go to worship the Lord with the *saints*, you will be able to say, "I am going now to see my God; I am going to worship my Lord. I will *not* go with empty hands but with hands full of *Christ*. I have a surplus, and in my right hand is the best part reserved for my dear Lord."

YOUR BEGINNING

What really happens to us when we believe in *Christ*? Let me list some of the gifts God gives you when you commit your life to *Christ*. This is not just for the new in *Christ*, but those that need re-fueling.

A NEW RELATIONSHIP

The instant we first come to God and we give our lives to *Christ, at that moment,* God gives us a new relationship.

Once we were separated from God because of our sins and not just separated, but alienated from Him. The Bible says we were "excluded, without hope and without God in the world." (Ephesians 2:12)

But *Christ* took away all our sins; not just part of them, but *all* of them! You are forgiven. The one thing that separated you from God [your sin], has now been removed, and therefore you are reconciled to Him. Instead of being God's enemy, you are now a part of His family. The Bible says, "Therefore, having been justified by faith, we have a peace with God through our Lord Jesus *Christ*" (Romans 5:1). We are His children.

The Bible uses two vivid images to illustrate this. First, it tells us we have been born again. A second image the Bible uses is adoption. If we have given our lives to *Christ*, God has adopted us into His family. He is now your loving heavenly Father, and you are now His child, spiritually born into His family.

A NEW CITIZENSHIP

God then gives you, after you commit your life to *Christ*, a new citizenship. You are still a citizen of a particular country, but now you are also a citizen of the Kingdom of God.

In Jesus' day, one of the most coveted privileges a person could have was Roman citizenship. A Roman citizen paid fewer taxes, and if he went into the army, he automatically became an officer. A Roman citizen couldn't be punished, tortured, or put to death by crucifixion (except in very rare cases, such as treason). If found guilty in a Roman court, he had the right to appeal directly to Caesar.

But Jesus said His followers possessed something far greater than Roman citizenship and that was citizenship in the Kingdom of God. In His first sermon, Jesus declared, "The time is fulfilled, and the kingdom of God is at hand. Repent, and believe in the gospel" (Mark 1:15). God's Kingdom, He made clear, wasn't an earthly political kingdom, but a heavenly spiritual kingdom. The *realm* over which God rules. The Bible says, "Our citizenship is in heaven." (Philippians 3:20)

As long as we are on this Earth, we possess dual citizenship. On one hand we owe allegiance to our nation and are called to be good citizens. But we are also citizens of the Kingdom of God, that Kingdom of which *Christ* is the head. Our supreme loyalty is to Him, and if someone demands we do wrong, "We ought to obey God rather than men" (Acts 5:29). And someday, the Bible tells us, this world's kingdoms will become "the *kingdoms* of our Lord and of His *Christ,* and He shall reign forever and ever!" (Revelation 11:15)

A NEW FAMILY

God also gives us a new family. You aren't just related to God; you are now related to other believers. Everyone who truly believes in Jesus *Christ* is now your spiritual brother or sister. We are bound together in God's family, not by an organization but by a spiritual relationship. The Bible calls us "fellow citizens with the saints and *members* of the household of God" (Ephesians 2:19). One of the most frequent terms for Christians in the Bible is "brothers," underlining our family relationship.

In my journeys, I have often met men and women who were very different from me. And yet after a few minutes it was almost as if we had known each other all our lives. Why? Because we both knew *Christ*. Our common spiritual bond cut through the barriers that separated us, and we enjoyed fellowship as members of God's family.

A NEW PURPOSE

When we come to *Christ,* God gives us a new purpose. We now want to live for *Christ* and not just ourselves. We begin to see other people differently, not for what they can do for us, but for what we can do for them.

The Bible says, "For we are His workmanship, created in *Christ* Jesus for good works, which God prepared beforehand that we should walk in them." (Ephesians 2:10)

When I came to Christ, I had little suspicion of what I might do with my life, but little by little I was beginning to have a new purpose in life: a desire to live for *Christ*. I was learning that "those who live should no longer live for themselves but for him who died for them and was raised again."(2 Corinthians 5:15)

A NEW POWER

One of the Bible's most comforting truths is that when we come to *Christ*, God Himself comes to live within us by His Holy Spirit. We are not alone; God is with us!

The Bible says, "If anyone does not have the Spirit of *Christ*, he does not belong to *Christ*" (Romans 8:9). If you know *Christ*, you don't need to beg for the Holy Spirit to come into your life; He is already there, whether you *feel* His presence or not.

But why has God given us the Holy Spirit? One reason is to help us live the way we should. God has given us a new purpose, but without a new power we'll never be able to achieve it. We are too weak.

The Bible says, "The Spirit helps us in our weakness" (Romans 8:26). Jesus promised, "But you shall receive power when the Holy Spirit has come upon you" (Acts 1:8). We aren't meant to live the Christian life in our own strength. God has provided His Spirit to help us.

A NEW DESTINY

The word conversion means 'change' and the most fundamental change of all when we come to *Christ* is that God gives us a new destiny. Once we were headed for hell; now we are headed for Heaven! Once we were bound for eternal separation from God; now we will live with Him forever! Once we had no hope of eternal life; now we do! The Bible says, "For the wages of sin *is* death, but the gift of God *is* eternal life in *Christ* Jesus our Lord." (Romans 6:23)

As noted in this verse it says: Eternal life is a gift. Many misunderstand this (even some Christians). They still think they must earn their salvation by their own good works.

We can *never* be good enough to earn our way into Heaven, because God's standard is perfection. Our only hope is *Christ*, who purchased our salvation at the cost of His own *blood* and now offers it to us as a free gift. The Bible says, "In his great mercy he has given us new birth into a living hope through the resurrection of Jesus Christ from the dead, and into an inheritance that can never perish, spoil or fade; kept in heaven for you" (1 Peter 1:3–4). What a precious gift!

A NEW JOURNEY

God gives us a new journey...a whole new path to follow until the day He *takes* us to Heaven.

In other words, your decision for *Christ* isn't an end but a beginning, the beginning of a whole *new* life. We aren't only called to become Christians; we are *also* called to be Christians.

Don't ever think that faith in *Christ* is just a type of "spiritual life insurance," something we obtain and then put away until we need it to get into Heaven. The Christian life is a new journey, one that will take us the *rest* of our lives. We never walk it alone, for *Christ* walks with us.

THE NEW BIRTH

Have you ever heard or even asked yourself this question: "What is new birth"? Nicodemus asked this question too: "How can a man be born when he is old?" He wanted to understand it.

How can we travel 66,000 miles per hour and rotate at a speed of 1,000 miles per hour and sustain a distance from the moon at around 133,000 miles and keep a distance 400 times that from the sun? I now understand it's *all* in God's hand as He created and controls *all* aboard the Spaceship Earth.

I didn't understand it, but I accepted it by faith. Of course now God has given me the knowledge to see it. We have to look beyond our realm and accept what is true. Nicodemus could see only the physical and the material, but Jesus was talking about the spiritual.

How is the new birth accomplished? We cannot inherit new birth. The Bible says that those who are born again "were born, not of blood, nor of the will of the flesh, nor of the will of man, but of God." (John 1:13) Our fathers and mothers may be the greatest born-again Christians in the world, but that doesn't make us born-again Christians, too. Many people have the idea that because they were born into a Christian home, they are automatically Christians. They're not.

We cannot work our way to God. The Bible says that salvation comes "not by works of righteousness which we have done, but according to His mercy He saved us, through the washing of regeneration and renewing of the Holy Spirit." (Titus 3:5)

Nor is reformation enough. We can say, "I am going to turn over a new leaf," or "I am going to make New Year's resolutions." But Isaiah said that in the sight of God, "But we are all like an unclean *thing*, And all our righteousnesses *are* like filthy rags; We all fade as a leaf, And our iniquities, like the wind, Have taken us away." (Isaiah 64:6)

Some of us have changed on the outside to conform to certain social standards or behavior that is expected of us in our churches, but down inside we have never been changed. That is what Jesus was talking to Nicodemus about. He said, "Nicodemus, you need changing inside," and only the Holy Spirit can do that. Being born from above is a supernatural act of God. The Holy Spirit convicts us of our sin; He disturbs us because we have sinned against God. And then the Holy Spirit regenerates us. That is when we are born again. The Holy Spirit comes to live in our hearts to help us in our daily lives. The Spirit of God gives us assurance, gives us joy, produces fruit in our lives and teaches us the Scriptures.

Some people try to imitate *Christ*. They think that all we have to do is try to follow Jesus and try to do the things He did, and we will get into heaven. But we can't do it. We may know the religious songs. We may even say prayers. But if we haven't been to the foot of the cross, we haven't been born again. That is the message Jesus is trying to teach us.

To be born again means that "[God] will give you a new heart and put a new spirit within you" (Ezekiel 36:26). "Old things have passed away; behold, all things have become new" (2 Corinthians 5:17). We are "partakers of the divine nature" (2 Peter 1:4); we have "passed from death *into* life" (John 5:24). The new birth brings about a change in our philosophy and manner of living.

THE MYSTERY

There is a mystery to the new birth. Jesus said, "The wind blows where it wishes, and you hear the sound of it, but cannot tell where it comes from and where it goes" (John 3:8) But you can see the result. Jesus did not attempt to explain the new birth to Nicodemus; our restricted minds cannot understand the infinite. We come by simple childlike faith, and we put our faith in Jesus *Christ*. When we do, we are born again.

CHRIST-LIKE

How do we become more *Christ*-like? It does not happen by accident, and it does not happen by force. God does not take away our free will and force us to change. Rather, we must turn to him and *seek* him. This is what the spiritual disciplines are designed to do. In prayer and study, worship and service, we make choices about what is a priority in our lives. We make choices each day about what god we will worship and serve.

Our desire is to be like *Christ,* to make decisions in the way He made them, to be fully dedicated to serving the true God. Paul told the Ephesians that our Christian goal is to "reach unity in the faith and in the knowledge of the Son of God and become mature, attaining to the whole measure of the fullness of *Christ*" (Ephesian 4:13). What an amazing goal.

In this life, we will not fully reach the perfection that is *Christ* and yet that remains our goal. The challenge does not dissuade us, does not make us give up. Rather, we *run* with patience the race set before us, for we know that if we continue faithfully, a crown of righteousness is assured for us. Even now, Paul says, we "are being transformed into his likeness with ever-increasing glory" (2 Cor. 3:18). Even the Corinthian church, with its visible problems, was in the process of being shaped by the Holy Spirit into the glory of Jesus *Christ.*

Are we being transformed? Scripture says that we are. Perhaps it seems slow, but it is still real. There is much more to come, of course we will be like *Christ* in his glory (Rom. 8:29; 1 John 3:2) , but Paul's point is that we are *already* being transformed into the likeness of *Christ.* He is already being formed in us. That is what salvation is all about: We give our lives to him on a daily basis, and he shapes us to become more like him. God is saving us for this very reason: that we become like his Son.

How is it done? In Colossians 3:9-10 gives us the answer: "You have taken off your old self with its practices and have put on the new self, which is being renewed in knowledge in the image of its Creator." Ephesians 4:22-24 gives a similar answer: "Put off your old self, which is being corrupted by its deceitful desires; to be made new in the attitude of your minds, and to put on the new self, created to be like God in true righteousness and holiness." Out with the old, and in with the new! Put off wrong ways, and put on the way of *Christ*. (Or rather, let *Him* put it inside you, so it is in your heart and not just a pretense.)

This is the lifelong job that we Christians have, a daily duty, a daily *joy* as we experience our true identity in *Christ*. Our life is centered on Jesus, who not only shows us the Father, he also shows us what *we* can be like as we follow him.

As *Christ*-like people, we have a *Christ*-like job. Jesus told his disciples, "Go and make disciples of all nations, baptizing them in the name of the Father and of the Son and of the Holy Spirit, and teaching them to obey everything I have commanded you" (Matt. 28:19-20). We are to teach the things he taught, to do the things he said to do, to believe the things he said to believe. That is our business, our job.

Our work begins at home, where we learn what Jesus taught and begin to obey him. And for most of us, we continue to work at home, in our families and in our neighborhoods. It is not possible for every Christian to go into the entire world, nor is it necessary for every believer to travel. Jesus' point was that we are not to restrict our work by ethnic group, nor by social class or gender. (Gal. 3:28)

People's lives *are* being transformed! The good news is being preached, and people are being baptized. People of all ages are coming to *Christ*, and in all this I rejoice.

Now, there is more work to do. We need to teach new believers what Jesus taught, not just in words, but also in our actions. Actions of grace and compassion, actions of worship and service. A *Christ*-like person is the salt of the earth, the light of the world, ready to give an answer, ready to make disciples. A *Christ*-like person teaches and obeys Jesus' commands, loving others, praying for others, helping others, and in doing so, will be living proof that we are following Jesus *Christ.* "By this all will know that you are My disciples, if you have love for one another" (John 13:35). and Pursue peace with all people, and holiness. (Hebrews 12:14)

We can be confident that God will *not* abandon us. He went to the extreme of sending his only Son to die for us;

we can be assured that he will not forget what he is doing in our lives. He is lifting us, changing us, transforming us to be in the God Family. We are His children, too, being created anew through the Holy Spirit, destined for glory, like *Christ* eternally! We have a *glorious* future and we have already begun to enter that glory. *Christ* is already being formed in us, and we are being transformed into his likeness with ever-increasing glory.

Let *Christ* be formed in you, and labor so that he may be formed in all the church. Let us be about our Father's business, seeking his will, seeking him. Let him change us for his purpose, and our glory will be his glory.

OUR WINDOW

We have a window of opportunity to search out the hidden purpose of our existence, to find our way back to God.

In short, mankind desperately needs to be reconciled to God. (Isaiah 59:1-14) It is our *sins*, our abandonment of

His laws, that stand in the way. Only when we repent of doing things contrary to God's instruction can we experience a true *relationship* with our Creator. We need to learn what He expects of us.

What does He advise us to do? "*Seek* the Lord while He may be found, call upon Him while He is near. Let the wicked forsake his way, and the unrighteous man his thoughts; let him *return* to the Lord, and He will have mercy on him; and to our God, for He will abundantly pardon. (Isaiah 55:6-7)

The Bible refers to what is advised here as repentance: turning from our ways of doing things and surrendering to God to begin living according to His ways. Each person who turns to God in repentance and faith will be *saved*.

God "now commands all men everywhere to repent" and forsake our self-induced ignorance. (Acts 17:30)

God wants to show us the *way out* of our hardships and miseries and grant us understanding of the amazing knowledge of His plan for us. "Call to Me, and I will *answer* you, and show you great and mighty things, which you do not know" (Jeremiah 33:3). He will reward those who *seek* Him with their whole heart. In our high-tech information age we sadly lack the most essential information of all—the *knowledge* of God.

God offers the help of His Church, the spiritual Body of believers He describes as "the pillar and ground of the truth" (1 Timothy 3:15). He encourages us to grow in the "grace and knowledge of our Lord and Savior Jesus *Christ.*" (2 Peter 3:18)

In summary, "Without faith it is *impossible* to please Him, for he who comes to God must believe that He is, and that He is a rewarder of those who diligently seek Him." (Hebrews 11:6)

Do you know that the spark plug of faith is praise? Praise the detergent which purifies faith and purges doubt from the heart. The secret of answered prayer is faith without doubt (Mark 11:23). And the secret of faith without doubt is *praise*.

As you continue 'on life's track' you will come across God's hurdles. You might have experienced smaller obstacles which Satan is allowed to put in our way, but God permits larger ones to confront us. God has promised some very wonderful rewards for the overcomers, and how can we become overcomers with nothing to overcome? Let us show all onlookers (to the glory of God) that we believe Romans 8:28 and Ephesians 1:11 when bad news is given us, and immediately began praising God that He is *big enough, powerful enough, and loving enough to take care of this new treat* in a way that will bring more glory to His Name.

GOD THE FATHER

Let's talk about God. Who is God? Probably the most misunderstood term in the world is the term for God. I believe that at the heart of most spiritual problems is the misconception of God. Much of religious heresy is the result of misunderstanding God. Daniel 11:32 says, "And those who know their God shall be strong, and carry out great exploits." When we come to properly understand God, then we can *trust* Him and see great things happen.

Yet here is a problem that keeps many of us from a proper relationship with our heavenly Father. Psalms 50:21 says, "You thought that I was just like you." We project on our Heavenly Father the image of our earthly father. If our earthly father did not spend time with us, it is hard to grow up and think "My Heavenly Father wants to spend time with me." If our earthly father would not listen to us, it is hard to think "My Heavenly Father wants to listen to me."

I thank God for the personal relationship He gave me to enjoy with the short time of my earthly father, Bob Mackey. I learned from my Dad to seek out the knowledge of everything possible and to excel in it. When I came to the 'crossroad' and made the *choice* to seek God, the experiences my Dad gave me and the instruction to excel played forth in the decision for me to join the race for *Christ.* This one is 'for you' Dad.

I have learned one thing over the years, my Heavenly Father is a lot different than my earthly father. Some of you may have had an earthly father that was an alcoholic, drug addict, work workaholic, or maybe abusive verbally and emotionally. The list can keep going onward as there are so many types of sinful addictions, but as a result you projected that upon your Heavenly Father, and that can cause barriers in truly coming to *Christ.*

Now the question is: Who is God? God has revealed Himself in the scriptures. He has revealed himself through showing us His attributes. An attribute is something that is true of God in His basic nature. So when we say God is loving, He is simply being Himself. Let's look at some of His attributes.

The first one is this: God has revealed Himself as being omnipotent, all powerful. Every time I see the word omnipotent I think, "He can do it." And the scriptures point out that "He ruleth over all the kingdoms of the heathen and nothing is too great for God." He spoke to nothing and something came into existence! Now how does this affect us in our personal life and walk with *Christ*? It allows me to pray for things that I would never dream of praying for if I didn't know He can do it. Second, when you are really tired, He gives strength to the weary.

A number of years ago I was going through a 'midlife' crisis. The week before I had to be packed and start a new journey, I realized how exhaustion was taken over me. And I sat there that Saturday morning and I started to weep. I just said, "God, I can't do it. I am so exhausted. I don't even have the energy to get up out of this chair." And I just said the most important thing, "God, please help me."

Something happened and strength came into me, I stood up, smiled and got to the packing. I probably exerted more energy for one hour than I had the whole week prior. Later, I said, "God, thank you, for you are able." I cannot tell you how many times in my life I have had to call upon that strength (Exodus 15:2). "The LORD is my *strength* and my defense; he has become my salvation. He is my God, and I will praise Him, my father's God, and I will exalt him."

The Bible says that God is not only omnipotent, He is omnipresent, all present. This is a phrase that I use, "He is here." That means there is no point nearer to God than any other point. (Psalms139:8,9,10) says, "If I ascend into heaven, You *are* there; If I make my bed in hell, behold, You *are* there. If I take the wings of the morning, And dwell in the uttermost parts of the sea, Even there Your hand shall lead me, And Your right hand shall hold me." God is immediately accessible *wherever* you are.

Now the Bible says to draw *near* to God. How can you draw near to God if there is no point closer to God than any other point? When it talks about drawing near to God, it is speaking of your experience, not your position. If you are in a relationship, then you are continually learning things. You are being drawn closer together, not physically in position, but emotionally in experience. When God says to draw near to God, He's not saying get closer physically in position but rather emotionally in your experience.

Then the Bible says that God is omniscient, meaning "He knows it." (Psalms 139:1-6) says, "O LORD, You have searched me and known me. You know my sitting down and my rising up;You understand my thought afar off. You comprehend my path and my lying down, and are acquainted with all my ways. For there is not a word on my tongue,

But behold, O LORD, You know it altogether. You have hedged me behind and before, And laid Your hand upon me. Such knowledge is too wonderful for me; It is high, I cannot attain it. knows every thought. God is just not the God of reality, He's a God of all possibilities."

Because of knowing that He's omniscient it helped me to make that decision in moving. I said, "God here's everything to my future. My life is yours." What helped make that decision so much easier is that I knew God knew all of the possibilities of my life and because He loved me, He *chose* the best.

I don't have any fear of any skeleton coming crashing out of the closet in my relationship with God. If there is any skeleton there God knows it. He's acquainted with all of the intimacies of my life. Because "He *knows* it", I have 'no fear' that there is some unknown weakness in my life that is going to destroy my relationship with God or Him ever using me. He knows all the weaknesses and He still *loves* me and uses me.

Then God is immutable. He never changes. (Malachi 3:6) says, "For I am the Lord. I do not change." His power can *never* diminish nor His glory ever fade. He will always be the same. This encourages me to pray, not thinking, "Today He might hear my prayers, tomorrow He won't." He is the same yesterday, today and tomorrow. I know every day He will hear my prayers if I come in purity and faith before Him. I do not have to worry if I am going to find God in a receptive mood or not. He never changes.

As human beings, we project our earthly relationships upon our Heavenly Father over scriptural truth. With many people today, the number one barrier to coming to Jesus *Christ* as Savior and Lord is the image of their earthly father. Because Like God said, you look at me altogether as you look at yourselves. And so one of my prayers is that as we go through who God is, He may be your father, but He's not your old man. He is totally different than our earthly father.

HIS IMAGE

God has a true desire for us to understand Him. He inspired His Holy Word and He inspires those who would speak of Him. In Genesis; God said "let Us create man in Our own image...."

We must know that God is a Spirit and not a physical being like you and me. In (John 4:24) we see: "God is a

Spirit: and they that worship him must worship him in spirit and in truth."

He did not create us to physically resemble Him but to *spiritually* resemble Him. Look around you at the physical types of human beings that exist in this world. If we are to think that our physical image is the image of God, which would be His image?

Jesus told His disciples in: (John 5:37) "And the Father who sent me has himself testified concerning me. You have never heard his voice nor seen his form." And in (John 14:7) "If you had known Me, you would have known My Father also; and from now on you know Him and have seen Him."

I believe Jesus is telling us that the *image* of the Father is a spiritual image. How do we resemble the creator? What did Jesus mean that if we have seen Him we have seen the Father?

Let's look into the image of God...

*The image of God is **love**.*

The image of God contains joy.
The image of God contains peace.
The image of God contains kindness.
The image of God contains patience.

God's image contains goodness.
God's image contains faithfulness.
God's image contains gentleness.
God's image contains self-control.

These fruits of the Spirit are just that. They are not gifts, they are fruits which we must bear. Just as an apple tree is formed from the seed of an apple and bears again that fruit in kind so then we, who are formed from the *seed* of God should bear the same fruits that He bears.

This is what Jesus was telling us. If you look at the life of Jesus when He walked on this earth, you can clearly see that He bore the fruit of God and thus portrayed the *image* of His Holy Father.

God created us in His image. Jesus told us that if we have seen Him we have seen The Father. Jesus' spiritual image was love, joy, peace, kindness, patience, goodness, faithfulness, gentleness and self-control. We are from the *same* seed. God created us this way to contain His image.

There will come a day of judgment for each one of us (none shall be spared this). Each of us, believer and nonbeliever will one day stand before the Throne of God. He will peer into our hearts looking to see His *image*. When He sees His image in us, He will say, "Well done My good and faithful servant".

God speaks to each of us. His wants us to know that He loves us. He is Our Heavenly Father and as a perfect father He wants only the best for us. He often will let us make our own mistakes so that we will realize that without His strength, without His Divine help, we *are* lost.

Isn't it good to know that we have a wonderful and forgiving Father who wants to see us grow in our relationship with Him. My prayer is that, by reading God's Word, your relationship with Him will deepen and grow to be rich and fruitful in your life.

GINGERBREAD MAN

I want to *share* with you the story of the little gingerbread man who was fashioned and shaped by a little boy to be his treasured companion. The boy loved the gingerbread man, but he didn't need him...he merely looked in on him every day. One day the gingerbread man ran off down the street. The little boy ran after the gingerbread man, saying, "Come back!" "You're mine!"

The boy looked all over town, in all the stores, and asked all the children, "Have you seen my gingerbread man?" Then he passed a pastry shop where he saw his little gingerbread man smiling down from the store window with a price tag of five cents on him. He rushed into the store and protested, "That's my gingerbread man. I want him back!" The baker said, "You can have him for a nickel."

The little boy responded, "But you don't understand, I made him! He's mine!" The baker replied, "Fine. If he's yours, pay the price and you can have him." So the little boy took a nickel from his pocket and paid for the gingerbread man. He gazed at him lovingly and said, "Now you're really mine. You were mine first because I made you, but now you're mine because I bought you."

The same is true with redemption. God says, "You were mine because I *made you*, but you ran away from Me. Now you're mine because I *bought you* with the *blood* of *Christ*." He has redeemed us.

The Lord stands at your door and He is asking that you quit running away. He wants you to be apart of the God family.

Are you tired of being in the dark? Right now is the time to come to the light of Jesus *Christ*, now...not tomorrow. If you are a believer and have strayed from God's path for your life, won't you confess your sins and come back to *Christ* today?

Are ready to leave the darkness, the fear, and doubt behind you? Won't you come to the His light and pray to Him right now:

Lord, I know I have been living my life in darkness. I have sinned against You, but I want a new life and from now on I want to live in Your light. I ask from my heart that you please forgive me and replace the darkness in my life and in my heart with the light of Your love. I surrender to You and ask Your Son, Jesus Christ, to be my Savior and Lord. Turning away from sin, I give myself to You. Guide me daily in the path of the light as You are in the light. Amen.

Jesus spoke to them again, saying, "I am the light of the world. He who *follows* Me shall not walk in darkness, but have the light of life." (John 8:12)

In unity we have enjoyed *sharing* the Word of God. I pray you continue to seek Him, draw upon His presence, and go forth with His light upon your *walk* with Him, in Him, as He walks the †Crosswalk path with you, as the Son of God has also walked.

†CROSSWALK MINISTRY

For the 'true' believing Christian, in *Christ,* we see that the cross is a wooden 'altar' upon which God sacrificed His Holy Word, The Spotless Lamb, to pay the sin debt of all who would receive it. There He bought redemption for all.

That same altar is the altar where we too can sacrifice ourselves to God. It represents: salvation, redemption, salvation, unity, and righteousness.

The members of †Crosswalk Ministry are committed to fulfilling Christ's admonition to carry the message of God's truth to the world and teaching people His way of life.

Robert Mackey of †Crosswalk Ministry is a writer and minister of God's Word and His creation.

May you find your peace with God. We are always here for you.

Email: crosswalkministry@live.com

www.crosswalkministry.webs.com

www.crosswalkministry.com

Crosswalk Ministry

PO Box 234, Broken Bow, OK 74728

Follow the path, stay in the race, and *keep* the faith.

Your attitude should be the same as that of

Christ Jesus

WHO, BEING IN VERY NATURE GOD,

did not consider equality with God something to be grasped,

BUT MADE HIMSELF NOTHING,

taking the very nature of a servant,
being made in human likeness.

And being found in appearance as a man,
he humbled himself
and became obedient to death —

even death on a cross!
- Philippians 2:5-8

Mackey

20332050R00080

Made in the USA
Lexington, KY
30 January 2013